Full Circle

the
creative
church for
today's
society

david r. mains

WORD BOOKS • Publisher • Waco, Texas

FULL CIRCLE

ISBN #0-87680-846-1
Library of Congress catalog card number: 77-181100
Printed in the United States of America.

Unless otherwise noted, all Scripture quotations are from the Revised Standard
Version (RSV) of the Bible, copyrighted 1946, 1952, © 1971, 1973 by the Division
of Christian Education of the National Council of the Churches of Christ in the
U.S.A., and are used by permission.

Quotations marked Taylor are from **Living Gospels,** by Kenneth N. Taylor, copy-
right 1966 by Tyndale House Publishers.

Dedicated
to Mr. Louis F. Peick
whose openness to union
with us has in many
ways made our labors
possible.

Contents

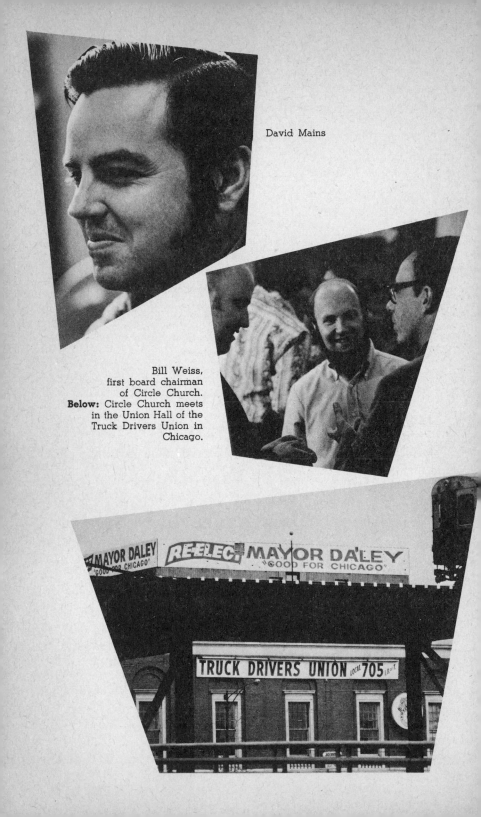

David Mains

Bill Weiss,
first board chairman
of Circle Church.
Below: Circle Church meets
in the Union Hall of the
Truck Drivers Union in
Chicago.

Introduction

As a young man venturing into the ministry, I was strongly advised by many sources not to get trapped in the limitations and frustrations of a pastorate. One associate went so far as to predict that local congregations with their prevailing problems would be dead in ten years' time. My response was, "If there is a chance that such a statement is even partially true, some of us must attempt to reverse the trend, because I see nothing on the horizon capable of replacing the local church."

Our modern age of dissent has pointed a devastatingly accurate finger at the inadequacies of today's church. Unfortunately the average book related to this theme has been lengthy in analyzing problems but surprisingly brief regarding solutions. Overwhelming criticism, both from within and without, has for too long now been heaped upon the church. The time has come when it is the responsibility of Christians who find such fault to begin the honest agony of reappraisal, which must continue until practical, imaginative, and biblical solutions to the problems are discovered. I refuse to believe that God will accept withdrawal as an answer, and nihilistic dissent is a great sin in the presence of His positive creative power. We must act in the patience and perseverance of His Spirit, until we can definitely ascertain that the church is once again setting the precedent for society rather than having society set the precedent for her.

Historically it is probably too soon to be recording the events of this Circle Church experiment. While I believe that in the four years of our existence the basic philosophy has solidified, I have also come to feel that one never finalizes the methodology used to implement established purposes. Therefore, my desires in writing this book are:

1. **To establish clearly the reasons for the existence of the local church.** Undoubtedly, the key problem of the traditional church today is that it lacks defined objectives. I feel, therefore, that the specific ideas about how a local church functions form the most critical part of this book. This material is not written about an urban parish exclusively; it relates to all congregations. I state this because I feel the dying church is **not** just a city phenomenon. This same lack of defined objectives is already beginning to take its toll in the suburbs.

2. **To suggest new methods by which the local church can fulfill her purposes.** I have intentionally chosen the word "suggest" because I do not believe our methodology is the answer to all problems. As one of our Board chairmen, Bill Weiss, stated, "We are not interested in establishing in McDonald Hamburger fashion a Circle Church franchise!" We do not have answers to all the problems **we** face, nor will the solutions which are satisfactory to us necessarily fit the personality of another parish. But we are a part of the explosion of creative forms and expressions that is occurring in the contemporary church. Possibly, just reading our ideas can trigger new thoughts regarding other situations. Perhaps for someone this book can be a starting force. I will be pleased if we can lend inspiration through our simple sharing. We believe all churches must grope with the philosophy presented in these pages. The outworking of the philosophy, the methodology, is not limited to what we have done.

3. **To illustrate these concepts by sharing what God is doing at Circle Church.** It is important not to think that methods are the sole key to what has happened in our Chicago setting. Obviously, God can supersede the poorest of plans. The vital aspect of the Circle Church story has been a combination of honest evaluation, clear direction, hard work, and **supernatural anointing.** This is why I have begun the book with illustrations of what God has brought about beyond our own efforts. I wanted to identify His part quickly before showing how philosophy and methodology are related.

This is a day when outstanding demonstrations of God's power are desperatetly needed. We say we are called of God, and then we quit before seeing Him carry us through. I am convinced we have given up too many battles God expected us to win. We are no longer men of daring. Circle Church was begun in a place where, to that time, no evangelical ministry had survived. We were attempting to prove some principles in which we believed strongly. If they worked here, no one could say, "Sure, you had it made before you started." The concepts are important, but they are not enough in themselves. What has carried us on are those times when, with our backs to the wall, we have cried out to God and He has seen us through. I hope this flavor comes out strongly. Circle Church is not our private possession; it belongs to God!

As a pastor, I am fulfilled and challenged and renewed by each moment of my exciting ministry. I love the church, even though institutionally she has grown horribly obese and immobile. I love her people, as confused as some of them seem to be. I love her leader, Christ, and want her to be beautifully clothed in the dignity of spiritual graces as He intended. I want the church to be strong as He would want—not with superficial power of property and worldly prestige, but with a living fire.

When Christ cleansed the temple, these words are recorded in John 2:15-17:

> And making a whip of cords, he drove them all, with the sheep and oxen, out of the temple; and he poured out the coins of the money-changers and overturned their tables. And he told those who sold the pigeons, "Take these things away; you shall not make my Father's house a house of trade." And his disciples remembered that it was written, "Zeal for thy house will consume me."

Those are my sentiments exactly! **Zeal for thy house—thy church —will consume me, O Lord.** We hope that we will continue to be a part of the cleansing God is performing throughout His work.

THE CIRCLE IS FORMED

I.

Above, left: Larry Mayfield took over the music direction from Sherm Williams. **Right:** Mel Warren was Circle's first black pastor. Clarence Hilliard (below left) took over from him. Ka Tong Gaw (below right) was the third to join Circle's staff in 1967.

Chapter One

"If you begin a new work, you are a fool!"

"If you are holding your own in a city church, it's a miracle. If you are slowly dropping behind, God is blessing. But if you begin a new work, you are a fool!"

There was no mistaking the intent of this minister's words. His analysis was factual and his advice sound. No precedent existed for beginning a new church in the inner-city, and there were certainly no guarantees of success. Nothing is more difficult to explain reasonably than the unreasonable leading of God, and there was no convincing this friend that our projected plans were anything but audacious.

I'm not sure I can claim that the anticipated step was totally one of faith—at the time it seemed to be the only option. I was employed by a large Chicago church as assistant pastor, and a new head minister had been called. In accord with custom, the staff members were considering tendering resignations and locating other positions. In a way I was glad, due to the considerable misgivings I was experiencing in this, my second job in the traditional church. My frustrations had reached the point where it was not uncommon for me to endure tension headaches on Saturday afternoon in anticipation of the Sunday services and not to find relief until after a good night's sleep following the evening meeting. Monday and the first half of Tuesday were fine, but the pressure soon returned with the approaching midweek service.

I first began to be concerned about churches while working as a Youth for Christ director. Being continually involved in the conversion and spiritual growth of teens, I found great difficulty in transferring that fresh vitality to the latency of the average church.

15

Only a few of the many pastors I knew mirrored the freedom, joy, and spiritual optimism I had come to associate with fellow YFC workers. Furthermore, I observed that evangelistic works were siphoning off a majority of the qualified seminary graduates, only serving to increase the desperate situation. It was a vicious cycle—an active, progressive, faith-inspired evangelism under well-qualified leadership unsuccessfully trying to feed into a dormant, reactionary, doubt-filled leaderless ecclesiasm, only to have converts soon leave the church and search elsewhere for the vibrancy they had originally experienced. It became clear that creative leadership would have to be channeled back into local congregations if total renewal was ever going to be experienced—but how could that be done? It was as a result of such reasoning that I eventually committed myself to a parish ministry.

Soon after taking my first job I discovered that, cursed as I am with an inquisitive mind and an open mouth, adjusting to a role as assistant pastor was not going to prove easy. To ask probing questions of the normal minister is to threaten his spiritual leadership, and to brainstorm new ideas with other members of the congregation is to be suspected of playing the traitor's role. If you function in a superior fashion—preaching well, ministering with love and, consequently, developing loyalty among the people—you arouse jealousy; yet if you perform inadequately—the youth group doesn't grow, or the Summer School is a flop—you are a sluggard. In short, you are damned if you do and damned if you don't!

Both churches with which I worked would be considered successful by normal standards. The first, a suburban parish of approximately 1,000 on Sunday morning, was made up of delightful people. On the whole, they were attractive, interesting, and cultured. Together they represented tremendous potential. Looking back in analysis, I feel they were involved in peripheral activities and had no conscious attitude of their real spiritual destiny—of what God could do through them as a group. Great amounts of their efforts went into the building itself. Typical was one Board meeting where these men, top executives in their professions, spent a long period of time deciding whether to purchase rubber floor runners or cocoa mats for the entrances in preparation for the oncoming winter season.

Prayer meetings were well attended, but the spirit of them did not reach my expectations, which probably mirrored Youth for Christ days when together on our knees, arms encircling one another, we pleaded for God to sustain our very existence. Somehow the oft-intoned reminders of missionaries around the world (in spite of a very active missions program), unsaved relatives, and the physically ill seemed manufactured. Rarely if ever, as I remember, were there requests that bared the open agony of a Christian in desperate need. Few seemed to be speaking from that precarious ledge called faith—striving in ministries, personal or congregational, so far above their familiar abilities that they required God's hand to keep them from falling. As a result prayer became cursory.

There was also a tendency for the group to be extremely in-grown. I taught a series in the couples' class (thirty-to-forty-year-olds) emphasizing the principle of developing non-Christian acquaintances—again another idea which evangelistic groups have developed and stressed. It was quite a shock to learn that not only did these warm, gracious people not have nonchurch friends, but that I myself, since leaving YFC, had become such a part of the church that I had not been developing these relationships either! The activity calendar had conspired against all of us.

I remember one conversation with a church leader who was knocking the "fundamentalists" for preaching so often against smoking. "Though no one mentions it here," he continued, "I can only think of one or two who attend who smoke, and I don't recall ever seeing a cigarette butt on the floor of the church, the vestibule, front stairs, or even in the parking lot!" His point was that outsiders were not likely to take advantage of this open-minded silence on the matter. I had never seen a cigarette butt in these places either. My point was: their very absence was not symbolic of the outsider's respect but of his disdain for our exclusiveness.

Transferring to Chicago after a little more than a year, I became assistant pastor of a ministry "known around the world" where, at that time, there was no head pastor. The auditorium alone seated over four thousand, and though the church had been declining, there was still an average attendance of close to nine hundred on Sunday morning. A strong tendency existed for the people to go back to "the good old days," when even the balcony was filled and "the best speakers from around the world" stood in the pulpit.

Their great craving was that someday a strong-voiced "deliverer" would come and lead them boldly back to yesterday! They were not interested in making plans even of a temporary nature until "Moses" appeared on the scene.

No one could accuse these people of being ambiguous about what they considered important when it came to church. Their single burning desire was to get people "saved." Every service terminated in an invitation regardless of what was preached. I remember one man who had made a covenant with God to lead someone to the Lord every day of his life. Sometimes he had to walk the streets late at night to make his contact and keep his oath! Once I asked him if any of these people had, after having made such a decision, started to attend the church. He responded that even though none had, he anticipated great joy in Heaven when he discovered what had happened to each one of the converts.

This man's sincerity was unquestionable, yet it seemed to me to be sadly out of balance. I, too, believe in conversion, but I hold that it must always be carefully presented in the total context of changing one's pattern of living. I don't believe it is possible for a person by good deeds to accomplish his own salvation. Neither, however, do I think it feasible to ask God for forgiveness while having secret reservations in regard to being willing, with God's help, radically to change one's life style. Interaction would have been very profitable for the total congregation at this point. The imbalance could have been corrected had the people been more adept at talking openly about such aspects of their faith, but the mind-set was such that this was not feasible. They interpreted someone's saying the same thing in a new way as bordering on heresy. To go further and listen openly and responsively to ideas different from their own—an impossibility!

Because evangelism was so important, the planned worship suffered. To me it was indescribably awful. The services were all alike. You knew exactly the ingredients and the order that would be followed even before you looked at the bulletin. To those who knew the in-language, they were invariably a "blessing" (I am still not quite sure what that word meant). The last-minute choice of Sunday night hymns and the assignments as to who did what part (I usually prayed for the offering) which were designated as we

stepped onto the platform were typical of countless churches I had
attended prior to coming here. All of this tended to make me
squirm uneasily during the ensuing hour and a quarter. Friends
insisted they actually visited the church for the specific purpose
of watching my discomfort! Though I was extra fidgety, they had
to admit it wasn't easy to sit under the preaching of a guest speaker
who, in 1966, emphatically proclaimed the impossibility of humans
ever setting foot on the moon because, according to the Bible, it
was God's territory!

By the time I was finally allowed to preach on a Sunday morning,
I had begun to doubt if I would ever be able to accomplish anything meaningful within the form of the traditional church. Early
that morning I asked God for a sign of His continued presence and
of confirmation regarding the direction I had taken in my life. The
remnant staff and I had decided to rearrange the service, placing
the announcements (which are always an anachronism to any
worship) before the call to worship so as not to interfere with the
flow of the service once it began. At the end of what I felt to be a
satisfactory morning, I extended the traditional invitation, but made
it of a precise nature, and was amazed when in a very brief time
thirty to forty walked to the front. My preaching ministry had never
been keynoted by exceptional altar response. Obviously God was
bending very near to me that morning, and His faithfulness made
me buoyant.

After the service I was made aware of a special elder's meeting
which had been hurriedly called. Naïvely expecting commenda-
tion, I was told in no uncertain terms that I was never again to
fiddle with the order of service without their approval! There was
no recognition of any spiritual deepening—thirty to forty people
who had been touched by God's Spirit—only an awareness of a
young staff member who was presumptuously trying to ruffle
tradition.

After a period of time, I began to content myself with working
in the high school department and was really not surprised to
discover how little these students paid attention to what was going
on. I gave them a primary level test with questions like, "Who had
the coat of many colors?" "What man built the ark?" "Name five of
Christ's disciples," etc. On a possible score of 100 the average of
the group was 17! When I gave these figures to the board of elders,

I was asked how this could possibly be since these young people were sitting under the finest preaching to be found. I in turn asked the men if any of them could tell me anything that had been said in a message over the last two months, including the previous Sunday. There was a long pause. I went from one man to the next, calling them by name, but none could remember anything that had been preached during that period in spite of the "big names" who were expounding each week.

The following Sunday one of the elders rushed up to me saying, "Brother Mains, I want to talk to you. I've been thinking about what you said, and I remember something from one of the sermons"!

Such confrontations did not make me the most popular person on the church staff. Once I began to be honest about my feelings, however, I had to come forth with all of the questions which were torturing me.

"Where as a church are we headed?" "Why do we always have a Sunday evening service?" "Do we have to hold all meetings in the building?" "Why are the announcements always right before the special number that has nothing to do with the sermon that follows?" "Why do we plan a Vacation Bible School, when we don't have enough people to staff it?" "Is it necessary to have a 5:30 Jet Cadet (youth group) Hour?"

Behind all of this probing was the basic question, "What is the purpose of this local church to begin with?" I found great frustration in being told, "Run, man, run! You're the person we really need to help the church out," when no one knew the ultimate destination much less the starting point.

There were occasions in the repetitious absurdity of services when I wanted to stand up and scream at the top of my lungs just to have broken the futility of it all! I must hasten to say at the same time that I was still deeply committed to Christ and continued to find Him meaningful in my life. I was exercising my gifts on a personal level, and with God's help maintained an active measure of love for the people with whom I worked, some of whom regularly demonstrated true concern for me in my struggles as well. Other nonchurch ministries were still open to me, and I found it difficult to continue imagining myself as a local church reformer. Yet what to do with the converts if I went back into an evangelistic outreach? That was the problem I had not been able to solve three years previously. Somehow a solution had to be found.

In the midst of the dilemma, a number of suburban pastorates opened to me, but the city had won my heart. I had become a captive of the old men wrapped in loneliness, seated on park benches; of the swinging, ardent young disciples of relativism and the Now philosophy; of the nameless humanity sifting through trash barrels; of the student masses, moving irrevocably beyond recall; of the sophisticated rich, resplendent with advantages, haunted by emptiness; of the minority poor, ensnared by incomprehensible poverty conditions; of the hippies and the professionals; of the politicians and the laborers. Unwittingly, my response had become that of Christ's—"when he saw the multitudes, he was moved with compassion . . . because they fainted, and were scattered abroad, as sheep having no shepherd" (Matt. 9:36, KJV).

No illusions existed for me as to the condition of the Protestant church in America's urban centers. Their position had been adequately chronicled by many authors. I knew such churches were few and far between and dwindling in size, and further I realized that many existing ministries were barely relating to the society which surrounded them, be it high rise or ghetto. Yet, I felt a lot like Harry Truman who reportedly kept a sign on his presidential desk which read, "The buck ends here."

We pastors have participated in passing the buck to explain the great problems of our twentieth-century cities. We've blamed political machines, the welfare dole, communist infiltration, or the inevitable moral decline of the "last days." But Scripture teaches **that if the salt disappears, decay will follow.** "You are the world's seasoning, to make it tolerable. If you lose your flavor, what will happen to the world?" (Matt. 5:13, Taylor). My conviction laid a great deal of the blame for urban perplexities at the foot of the fleeing church which had been unable to reconcile her traditions with the crises of humanity. Cities desperately needed a generous sprinkling of salt, shaken by the hand of God, that would position the positive influence of Christians in every nook and cranny of their crowded existence. The buck ended with us.

Yet nothing in the city opened for me, and the new minister had come. As I had expected, our thought patterns were quite different! The next few months were spent in an agony of reappraisal as I sought direction regarding a move. I read every contemporary book on the subject of church renewal that I could find and was especially impressed by the writings of Elton Trueblood. My wife and I ate and breathed church. There were nights when I could not sleep because of my concern, and our Old Town (a hippie and commercial night spot center) apartment became the scene of many wee-hour dialogues. Karen once peevishly insisted that we were not able to talk of anything **but** church. I challenged her and vowed not to mention a word about church for the rest of the evening. **We passed the next few hours in absolute silence!**

As time went on, it became quite apparent that there would not be a city church open to the kind of ideas so dear to me. If the church was large, it was successful in its own eyes and didn't feel a need for critical analysis. If it was small, it was probably because the people were the same way and they would not be open to what was going on in my mind.

Fortunately, seeds of dissatisfaction were blowing elsewhere, and soon a small core of friends had formed to share the conflicts and frustrations common to our ecclesiastical experience. We all lived in the city, but our conversations did not settle exclusively around the inner-city church. Our concern included the local church as a whole. Our despairs were a classic microcosm of the younger generation's anguish. We had reacted to the meaninglessness, the superficiality, the emptiness of our experiences. Yet we were determined not to drop out, not to conform to the Christian nihilism which maintained that nothing could be done for the church, that she was doomed.

Soon the criticism began to take on positive aspects. Thought-provoking questions were asked: "Well, if these are the problems common to our various experiences, how can we change them? If we could begin anew, what form would the church take? What was the New Testament church like, and can we find the secret of her vitality?" It was great fun!

Inevitably, probably because my open mouth dominated so many of these conversations, the question came (from Ed Elliott): "David, if we promise to support a new work in the city that would be free to pursue this thinking, would you be willing to pastor it?"

There was no excuse now for complaint without construction. If we could expend the energy in dissent, we could also expend the energy in action.

Some years back my wife and I had balked at the city's crime, its polluted air, its crush of population, its inadequate public schools, its explosive racial combinations. Yet, no ministry in the world can be successful without identification and personal involvement. Feeling strongly that the challenge was from God's Spirit, we decided that our home would remain in windblown, crime-ridden, panic-touched, but magnificent Chicago!

Certain practical qualifications had to be met before we could begin our venture. Six friends were hardly enough to merit another church. We needed a broader base from which to act. It would be necessary to locate a meeting place. The establishment of any new work, be it a business or a church, is loaded with frustrations, and I did not want to add that of part-time employment. Financial support for our family of four would be necessary. I would have to terminate my present responsibilities. We believed that if God truly was constructing our ambitions, then each one of these requirements would be met with that perfect clockwork timing we had come to identify with His leading.

Starting with the acquaintances of our small group, we eventually made contact with fifty people who carried the same burden for the present church and who had enough daring to step out in what was humanly a "foolish" effort. We were cautious not to draw people from my present employment. Of the fifty, I don't believe more than half joined with us when we actually began. Fortunately, our foresight was unaware of these statistics. Had we known, we might never have started. The group was for the most part composed of young white couples, many still in college or graduate training, most of them at this stage in life struggling to make ends meet. The larger percentage had not yet affiliated with existing churches, and their backgrounds were varied and diverse.

An erroneous concept exists in many minds as to the nature of the inner city. One soon discovers that its heart contains a large number of these intellectually gifted, potentially or presently well-to-do professionals whose cultural savvy views commuting, two-car garages, and small town concerts with obvious disdain. Still we deliberately attempted to locate the new work in a neighborhood that contained a cross-section of both worlds, the slum and the high rise, and in an area where no evangelical influence existed.

Certain prerequisites were established. We hoped to locate close to one of the expressway systems in order to facilitate travel to and from services, and we preferred eventually to have a place of our own that would give us visual exposure from such a major artery. We had to be near a student population, and certainly in a location that would be a cross-section both racially and culturally.

In December a date was set for beginning—the first Sunday in February, 1967. I was ready to give notice of resignation, when a call came from the Duncan YMCA on the near west side stating apologetically that plans had changed and the room for which we had made arrangements was no longer available on a weekly basis! In haste we located an old public grade school in the same neighborhood and made inquiries about renting the gym. It was available!

Sherm and Marti Williams, who had been a part of the core group from the beginning, accompanied me on an inspection tour. We walked into a time-worn room, overused by many children, dirty with age and strangely accented by weird patterns of daylight shining through the myriad broken windowpanes. Standing forgotten in the corner was a dilapidated piano. Marti, an accomplished pianist, ran her fingers over the keys. The sounds emitted must have been blasphemy to her trained ear. I am sure that one note in every octave was missing, and the middle C stuck whenever touched. Marti's next words typified the whole sentiment of those days. "It's all right," she smiled. "It will do!"

If God wanted us to begin in these surroundings, we were perfectly willing to do so and with thankfulness for His provision. Imagine my shock when I was notified by the Board of Education that the charge would be $172.50 per Sunday!

We combed our chosen neighborhood again and found nothing. It was now the final Friday afternoon of the year, and I had promised to give a definite answer to the new minister about the question of my future by Sunday, January 1. The deadline loomed closer and closer. Had God been leading us after all? Perhaps we were not exercising faith at all but had been presumptuous in attempting such an effort. Should I resign when there was a real chance a meeting place could not be found?

A quiet irritation with God began to nag at me. This was no
way for Him to treat someone who was climbing out on such a
precarious limb for Him! Pulling off the Eisenhower Expressway,
I vowed to look just one more time. Traveling west on Van Buren
Street, I noticed a large red brick building, neat and clean. I had
seen it before, but now in the quarter of the door window perched
a sign declaring, "HALL FOR RENT." It had been placed there that
afternoon!

The male receptionist was reluctant to show me the premises as
it was past closing time, and told me to come back Monday. In
desperation I did something which is naturally abhorrent to me. I
pulled rank and told him that I was a busy Reverend! It's hard to
cuss out a minister, and so he had me escorted upstairs where we
emerged into a cavernous ballroom. Ornate plasterwork encircled
the ceiling, and a highly polished wood floor stretched to the platform where a grand piano, antiqued in French provincial white,
reposed. The seating capacity was seven hundred, a thousand if
the balcony was utilized. My guide demonstrated the public
address system and informed me that the building belonged to
the International Brotherhood of Teamsters, Local 705, who had
purchased it from the Plasterers' Union.

"Is there anything smaller?" I inquired, and he steered me first
to an adjoining bar room. "Do you have anything else smaller?"
I persisted. He led me to the carpeted ladies' lounge. It could have
seated our entire group!

Arrangements for the hall were handled by Mr. Louis F. Peick,
the Secretary-Treasurer of Local 705. Entering his office, I distinctly
remember noticing the three spotlights which glared down on his
desk. Mr. Peick is one of the top labor negotiators in the city of
Chicago, and he was ready to go home. We talked briefly, but as
I explained our project, I sensed that I was not impressing him
with its urgency or importance. Gruffly he asked me what I thought
we could pay for the facilities. An instant replay of the horrible
gymnasium at $172.50 a Sunday flashed on. I gulped and asked
him to set the price.

My nervousness was not alleviated by the personage before me.
Louis Peick is tough in the manner of many big city officials, and
he has worked his way through the ranks to the top of a most
powerful union. Rising with a great laugh from his seated position

he said, "Young man, any time you want to start a church in this area you are welcome to come here and meet free! Do you think you could pay the janitor his wages?" He must have noticed my jaw bouncing off the floor. Just before I left, and with deep sincerity, he uttered the final coup de grace. "What this neighborhood **needs,** young man, is another God-damned Protestant church!"

Completely dumbstruck, I drove around the block to make sure of where I was. It would be just my luck to come back and not be able to find it again. In the back sprawled a huge parking lot. In a city of premium parking space, that was too good to believe. My wife maintains that when God gives a gift, He is careful to wrap it with all the extra trimmings. My gratitude had no human expression, and I was a definite hazard returning on the expressway with tears of thankfulness and relief blurring my line of vision.

The Union Hall sits between Ashland and Paulina Streets on the north side of the Eisenhower Expressway in the midst of great contrasts. Across the expressway and to the east looms the burgeoning University of Illinois Circle Campus. Named for the Circle interchange where the major arteries of the city meet, this recently constructed school is a triumph of modern architecture. It is presently said to be the fastest-growing university in the country, with an enrollment of eighteen thousand. Close by its side and directly south of "our" building lies the sprawling West Side Medical Center. The largest in the world, the Center is a complex combination of specialized hospitals, clinics, schools, dormitories, and personnel residences. One out of every five doctors practicing in the United States supposedly does some part of his training here.

To the rear of the Union Hall begins Chicago's famous westside black ghetto with Madison Street, Chicago's Skid Row, snaking along its inner boundaries and then moving toward its heart. It was in this area that the riots following Dr. Martin Luther King's assassination erupted, with great clouds of smoke rising from blocks burning about a mile from the Hall. In this area, Fred Hampton, the Black Panther leader, was killed during a highly disputed police confrontation. Malcolm X University is also located just one block to the west. A small ethnic Greek commercial district nestles eight blocks directly east. Our immediate neighborhood is 85 percent black, 10 percent Puerto Rican, and 5 percent Appalachian or poor white. As far as we could tell, there was no existing evangelical church witness in the area.

Because of the predominantly youth/student status of the core group, it was impossible to guarantee a secure financial salary. Some of us had been saving our tithes for several months, but the "pot" was not very large. Still, since God had led completely in every other area, I decided to trust Him for our livelihood. Karen, however, who is less inclined toward the mystical, agreed to provide day-care for Bruce, a three-month-old infant. Her explanation for this extra responsibility was that it was a ministry to the struggling grad student and his wife who had been hard pressed to find trustworthy care. We both knew, though, that she was taking practical measures to insure our continued eating. When our needs were faithfully met month after month, the extra funds were used for hospitality purposes.

A new congregation was ready to begin. Our purpose was to test ideas related to how a local church functions. What has unfolded is not only the story of an urban ministry, although many of the related circumstances are uniquely inner-city. It is a story of church renewal.

I maintain that the death of the city church has resulted from the same problems now being faced by most suburban churches. It has been apparent that the growth of many of these outlying churches can be attributed not to great numbers of conversions, but to the mobility of our society, as Christians move from place to place or exit from changing urban areas. We felt that if the theories we wished to test would work in the city with its obvious disadvantages—the great cultural diversities, the prohibitive costs of property, the changing neighborhoods, the shortage of Christians, and the consequent economic deficiencies—they would work anywhere! On the human level, we did not have a ready-made situation, but God had obviously prepared the way.

Chapter Two

*"God's in His heaven—
All's right with the world."*

Circle Church, originally named after its geographic location near the Circle Campus of the University of Illinois, began on schedule the first Sunday in February 1967, in the midst of the biggest snowstorm Chicago has ever experienced. Twenty-three inches fell in twenty-nine hours over January 26 and 27! By "our" Sunday, and the final day of snowfall, the total eleven-day accumulation was 36.5 inches!

For some reason, in the excitement of the new experiment it just didn't seem to matter that much. Creeping carefully along the hazardous streets, we passed one of our couples spinning their wheels trying to pull out from the curb. Faced with the real possibility of becoming immobile Good Samaritans on this, the first meeting of our new church, we contented ourselves with waving as we drove by, but that was all. We were stopping for nothing, snow-covered stop signs included. We made it, but they didn't.

Despite the great storm of '67, our attendance was twenty-eight. Our Christian Education facilities were in the nearby barroom and our nursery was in the ladies' lounge. It was an inauspicious beginning, to be sure, but because of the love and purpose shared, we were unaware of that.

Our memories of this beginning time are fond. Often the union would rent the hall on Saturday nights to various groups that would hold large and riotous parties. A few of us would arrive early the next morning to clear out the chaos so that we would have a relatively unlittered place in which to worship. Once the call telling us that there had been a party the evening before failed to come. When we arrived, the room was littered with one

28

hundred party tables covered with the refuse of the night before. Rolling up our sleeves, we pushed the confusion aside and cleared a small corner around the piano. The first hymn was one of praise, "This is my Father's word. . . ." With the fumes of liquor floating around us, with the shambles of cigarettes, leftover dinners, and torn paper cloths cluttering our surroundings; with the unhappy world outside, broken glass littering its sidewalks and grime staring from every corner of its streets, we sang ". . . and to my listening ears, all nature sings and round me rings the music of the spheres."

Often the Teamsters would hold meetings on the heels of our services, and we found ourselves the objects of their puzzled stares. Such strange juxtapositions—the go-go dancers of the night before or the rough-and-tumble Teamster policy meetings, and our little group quietly worshiping in a corner with bowed heads and open Bibles. The contrast of faces was incongruity in itself: the Circle Church people, young and hopeful, idealism and openness unabashedly there for all to read; the Teamsters, heavy-jowled and world-aware, an agony of expression written in facial lines and planes and muscles. How animal-huge they loomed to us! What must we have seemed to them? Besides which, our miniature Volkswagens looked ludicrous parked next to their armada of quiet black Cadillacs, powerful Pontiacs, and impressive Olds.

One Sunday morning, with the hodgepodge of disorder from the night before still in evidence, Mr. Peick wandered upstairs. He took one look, mumbled something to the custodian about "letting my people meet in this mess," and disappeared downstairs. Since that time the hall has always been clean and shiny when we enter. Often, on his order, men come at two and three o'clock in the morning to clean the hall for the "church service the Reverend has tomorrow morning." Despite the unpredictability of those days, we are thankful for each unusual moment of them.

Many parallels exist between establishing a business and establishing a church. The main similarity seems to be that in both ventures it is necessary to employ every resource—physical, emotional, financial—to its fullest potential. We gave every extra penny that we could, and we know that most of the people involved were living on the fine edge of insecurity themselves. After waiting years to hear me preach regularly, Karen found herself committed to children's church, Sunday school, and nursery responsibilities.

In the first nine months she attended very few morning services. It was strictly a do-or-die effort. Every weekday morning at 7:00 little baby Bruce would arrive at our doorstep. That was often before our own two sleepyheads had arisen. Karen might be expecting people for a pancake breakfast or for a sit-down dinner—we had guests in our home constantly. After the first two months we figured that we had entertained over two hundred people for one meal or another. Had we been pulling alone, it might have become unendurable, but we were aware of the combined strength and assistance of the total group. Each one of us was keenly conscious that our very existence was precarious. Yet we wanted so much for this precious dream to succeed, and the bond created by our efforts has left us very close indeed.

Our growth physically was steady but not phenomenal. In fact, on Labor Day weekend in 1967 (seven months after beginning) we were twenty-eight again! Contrary to normal city church patterns, in five more months we reached one hundred fifty and had registered two hundred by September of 1968. Even to the present, there has never been a morning service, but one, without visitors. (The exception was the Sunday following the rioting precipitated by Dr. Martin Luther King's death, when the National Guard patrolled our streets.) The visitors have usually come because they have been invited by friends. We have no roadside sign reading, "Jesus Saves," to identify our location (if any banner flies, it usually proclaims, "Vote for Mayor Daley"), and there has been little publicity or visitation initiated by ourselves. Consequently, because we have built the congregation on spontaneous personal invitations, the congregation is usually 8 to 10 percent nonchurched.

The average age of the group is slightly under thirty, and about 15 percent who attend are nonwhite. Our first two baby dedications were a beautiful illustration of this mixture; each time three sets of parents presented their children to the Lord—one white, one black, and one Chinese. We differ from one another in background and economic status, in ethnic and cultural experience, and in educational training. Some are new converts, while others were raised in Christian homes. Children account for about 10 percent of the congregation. Two-thirds of us live within a ten-mile radius of the Union building, and because the expressway system is at our door, a number come from the suburbs. Students from Circle,

Roosevelt, the Medical Center, the University of Chicago, Illinois
Institute of Technology, even Northwestern in Evanston, and many
other colleges attend regularly. Church-related or religious schools,
including Moody Bible Institute, North Park College, Emmaus Bible
School, and distant Wheaton and Trinity Colleges are often represented. After several months of operation, we affiliated with a
denomination, the Evangelical Free Church of America,* and have
been happy with the relationship.

As the days passed, an alternate choice demanded our attention.
Either we could have a part-time staff and a full-time building, or
a part-time building and a full-time staff. Because the Teamsters'
hall was adequately meeting our needs and the cost of urban
properties is quite prohibitive, we chose at this point to place our
emphasis on manpower. In September of 1967 we forfeited any
immediate plans for property when the church voted to take Sherm
Williams on the staff part-time to direct the music program. On a
volunteer basis he had built our miniscule choir from the miniature
congregation to a size too large to tuck behind the piano in the
corner of the auditorium from which we conducted the services.
The group of from fifteen to twenty, sometimes nearly as large as
the audience, now sang from behind the congregation. Unintentionally, we discovered that this simple adjustment enhanced our worship. Personalities no longer interfered with the message being
sung. Musically gifted, the choir always sings a cappella, and
this harmonious blend of voices floating across us as we worship
is a unique and satisfying experience. Occasionally soloists will
sing from this position also.

Taking Sherm on staff by no means indicated that our finances
were now stable. The church has never had an excess. In review-
ing some of the carbons of my early correspondence, I discovered
these lines:

> Regarding finances, with Sunday's offering we cleared
> the salaries due at the end of last week with a balance of
> about a dollar and a half. This meant we had to pay taxes

---

*The Evangelical Free Church is a small, 50,000-member fellowship of autonomous
Protestant churches, with headquarters in Minneapolis, Minnesota. Trinity Evangelical
Divinity School in Deerfield, Illinois, is under its jurisdiction. "Free" refers to its
European origins—such congregations remained free of the State church.

to the government today (Tuesday) of $654.00 with no money to do it. As of this morning, however, $656.00 has come in the mail. We have made it with pennies to spare, once again!

That paragraph is typical of what seems to be the Circle pattern. Our financial obscurity used to drain me until I discovered meaning in Christ's words in Matthew, "Seek ye first the kingdom of God and his righteousness; and all these things shall be added unto you" (6:33, KJV). I determined that if there was worrying to be done, God would have to do it. My responsibility would be to seek first His kingdom and then expect Him to supply our needs.

A month after Sherm became half of the two-member team, one of the key Board members, Ka Tong Gaw, notified us he would be leaving. A dynamic Chinese from the Philippines in his middle twenties, Ka Tong was a real spark in the congregation. He seemed to have the energy of ten men. The closest comparison I can make of his personality is to that child's toy, the Superball. The more it bounces, supposedly, the higher it goes, continuing and rejuvenating vitality. Working with internationals in the Chicago Loop, he was experiencing difficulty within his organization and had decided to return to the Orient with his family.

We had already become accustomed to people leaving. Our mobile culture, student transients, and the urban setting all conspired together to produce farewells with continuing frequency. How well I remember talking to our first Board chairman about the large number moving away, only to have him tell me he had just been transferred to New York! That calendar year we were to lose four successive Board chairmen! It was at the October Board meeting in 1967, our first year, that Ka Tong said his goodbyes.

Afterward, Sherm and I stayed to talk with him. How beautiful it would be if he could work for Circle Church. His foreign student contacts were phenomenal. His own background had prepared him perfectly to understand their difficulties and unique problems. At this point, Ka Tong had ready access, as well, to the ears of the foreign student advisors in the various universities. Not only was he unusually equipped, but our neighborhood was ready-made for this kind of ministry. At the University of Illinois schools in the Medical Center—less than five blocks from our meeting hall— there were over four hundred fifty graduate-level international students. In addition, Cook County Hospital, in our front yard, had over four hundred Filipino nurses alone. At Circle Campus there were over three hundred internationals. We had all heard of India's closing door to missions, but at the Illinois Institute of Technology on Chicago's near south side three hundred of their six hundred international students were from India!

Ka Tong was warm to the idea, but as a Board member, he was not ignorant of the church's financial picture. Personally I was feeling more and more certain that God wanted him to be a part of all that was happening. That's why I boldly asked him to attend the November Board meeting as well. Making noisy assurances that a miracle was going to take place, and finding nothing happening as the days passed, I felt pressured to do something I had never done before. I began to fast, asking God to make provision for Ka Tong's salary. Eating only one small meal a day (not being of spiritual giant proportions yet) and informing no one of my plan, I began the experiment on a Thursday. By Wednesday of the following week, God was to have done his work so that I could make a grand announcement as the Board met again that evening.

By Wednesday not a penny had come in. I was obliged to go to a ministers' breakfast, and although I attempted to arrive late in order to miss the meal, they were running behind schedule and I had to eat anyway. The prospect of having to forego supper made it a long, hungry day. The evening Board meeting came and went. The phone rang a couple of times and my heart leaped quickly, because I was sure it was some wealthy man burdened by God to underwrite this need. Once it was Karen's mother and the other time one of those helpless individuals in every ministry who desperately needs to talk and talk without purpose and without reason. Karen served brownies—crumbly rich, chocolately sweet —how good they looked! God seemed to be adding insult to injury!

Finally, when everyone was gone, Ka Tong turned to me as he was putting on his coat. "By the way, Dave, what was the big announcement you had me come to hear?" My self-imposed tribulation had not worked patience. I could have hit him.

It was 10:30 and I had had it. I went into the kitchen to eat and then stubbornly thought, "No, God. I'll show you. I'll go this whole blame week on nothing but one skimpy meal a day and prayer!"

At midnight I ate like a horse and still remember having two distinct reactions. First, my stomach hurt terribly, and second, I had a great inner peace that I had done all I could.

Within an hour of awakening the next day, I had two phone calls. The first was from "The Chapel of the Air" radio broadcast, and the conversation centered around possible projects for their mission outreach. I shared the prospect of Ka Tong's foreign student work, and they pledged $100 a month. The other call was from a young fellow in the congregation who asked me to meet him downtown. He had known of my burden about Ka Tong and expressed an interest to help. Reluctantly, I agreed to meet him. To me, it really was no longer that big a matter, because the battle had already ended.

Since the money had not been provided by the time schedule I had established, and it wasn't likely that a large pledge would be forthcoming from this person, I was once again irritated with God. I confess I have always had to overcome a rather obnoxious fixation that God answer my requests with nothing short of a "fireworks display." He is constantly confounding my ostentation by insisting on working in the way He chooses. For instance, I had been preaching in a suit where a hole had been worn in the seat of the pants. Karen carefully patched it, but obviously I needed a new suit. My preference would have been for a mysterious, anonymous letter containing the exact amount of a Brooks Brothers suit to have provided my need, rather than for my parents to tell me how sloppy I was getting, that they couldn't stand it any longer, and would I please, for heaven's sake, go charge one on their account.

Of course, the mysterious letters do come, but not when we are looking for them; and then our attitude is often, "Isn't this curious? What a coincidence." God is forcing me to take all things as from His hand, whether it be the expected paycheck, the junk that my wife discovers and from which she then creates beauty, the needs our parents see and fill. They're all miracles, and we are learning to be thankful for each one.

In spite of my irritation, I met the young man in his Loop office, and he pledged $350.00 per month. Overwhelmed, I called Ka Tong, and we met in the back booth of the Mayflower Doughnut Shop across from the Picasso on Dearborn Street. I told him the story I couldn't reveal the night before. He was quite impressed and said he would now pray about whether he should stay or not. Miracles, miracles, miracles—and he had to pray about it!

Not long afterwards, Ka Tong was in a small prayer circle with some friends not from the church group. While they were quietly praying, without warning and expectation he began to speak in tongues. This was not a normal occurrence in his life. Everything was very quiet and then an interpretation was given by a man who knew nothing of the situation: "God says He has opened the door for you. Do not fear to walk through it."

Now it was Ka Tong's turn to call me! God was at work. There were three of us now. A team was beginning to form.

One of the great lessons we were learning was to walk by faith. I am quite confident that many churches have resources so great in the human sense they no longer need God. We often joke within the group that Circle Church is held together by a few paper clips, a little Scotch tape, and a wad of gum. In actuality, we were constantly finding ourselves forced to pray, because we had immense needs. Later, as the church began to solidify and more finances were available, we found that our prayer began to drop off. There is a real spiritual secret to forcing yourself to live in the area of faith so that it is impossible to accomplish what needs to be done apart from God's help. This, in a very real sense, is what was happening. Stepping out in faith and praying that God would sustain us, we were finding ourselves divinely upheld.

In January of 1968 Sherm shocked me with this statement: "I've prayed about the matter and finally feel certain that God would have Marti and me take the job in Florida." A great broom seemed to be continually sweeping us to the four corners of the earth. Of the initial group of nearly thirty, one couple had left to go into missionary radio work in Alaska; one single fellow had accepted a teaching position in Beirut; Ed and Ginny Elliott, who were so instrumental in helping us bat out our basic philosophy, had moved to take a position of Christian Education Director in Michigan; and the one older couple, Bob and Mary Louise Niemeyer, who were in their later forties and had lent great qualities of stability to us, were transferred to executive positions in New York City. David Ying, M.D., had finished his residency at Presbyterian–St. Luke's Hospital and was preparing to activate his duties in the armed forces.

Everytime we turned around it seemed as though this single person had taken a different job or finished nurses' training. We could have bought farewell tokens by the dozen.

And now it was Sherm! Some years previously, when I had been the director of Fox Valley Youth for Christ and a part-time member of the YFC International Staff in Wheaton, Illinois, he had been a high-schooler. I invited him to be the music director for a rally we were planning, and that had been the beginning of a relationship which has sustained itself. We had laboriously discovered the boundaries of aggravation in one another, carefully explored the shifting moods of our contrasting personalities, and established a stable groundwork of mutual understanding and respect. It was hard not to be selfish and say, "I need you, don't leave me." It was continually a temptation to take each departure personally rather than determining to see the hand of God leading each individual lovingly and distinctly. Sherm had been offered a leadership position which included on-the-spot training in religious television. The organization wanted him and no one else. It was an undeniable opportunity for a young man in his twenties.

Because we remain in a very mobile situation, I am still not sure I see clearly God's reason for this constant dispersion. It remains hard to continue letting go of people you have come to love. It is difficult not only to say, "God bless you, go in peace," but to feel it. Somehow I am managing more and more to accept this all as from God's hand. Of course, the people who left were always replaced by several others. In the light of the Circle experiment, we have watched with intense interest the progress of those who have moved. We have seen them multiply themselves again and again in their chosen areas of ministry or in the churches with which they have affiliated.

Sherm's intense interest in Circle Church was demonstrated by his hand-picking a successor. Consequently, we began the second year of Circle Church with Larry Mayfield as a member of the staff. Larry and his wife Diane are both graduates of Moody Bible Institute, and he has completed his master's degree in trombone with work accumulating toward a doctorate. The two are the type you look at and say, "There are a couple of swingers!" Larry's sideburns, collection of rainbow-hued shirts and slightly mod style were as welcome as his music.

The choir flourished under Larry's direction, and the enthusiasm produced two major concerts a year. A small madrigal group was formed for those with a special interest in that type of sound. The music of Sunday morning is undoubtedly one of the major factors contributing to our growth. A great variety is employed from Bach to rock, but it is always done well and in the proper context. I don't know when I began to notice it, but soon sideburns began to appear more and more throughout the congregation on cheeks that were clean-shaven before. Larry was making himself known in more ways than one!

The second summer was hard again financially. I state that to relate briefly another story of the way the people of the church demonstrated their great concern for what was taking place. At the time, we were renting office space in an old Music and Arts Building in the Loop which has since been razed. The three families which had supported the work the most had moved. Salaries were already late and the office rent was due. Everything else was progressing well. We were all growing spiritually and the bonds were extremely close, but the finances were a hazard. One afternoon, a young father in the congregation told me he believed God was putting his dedication to the test. Knowing about the summer difficulties, he had withdrawn his savings and wanted to contribute $1,000. We literally would not have made it through the summer without his sacrifice.

In September, only one-and-a-half years old, we topped two hundred and were beginning to be concerned about this unexpected mushrooming. The facilities at the Union Hall are large enough to service growth, but we wondered what kind of effect this increase would have on the intimacy which the congregation shared. It was easy to slip into a kind of psychology which almost resented newcomers because of the intrusion they represented and because of the effort it required to attain in-depth knowledge of them. All along, we had generally conceded that two hundred would be a maximum figure of growth, and from that point we would branch out. I remember specifically preaching that it seemed more feasible for God to use many such vital lights around the city rather than one great beacon in a given location. When we experienced rapid growth, we felt it was now time to divide.

Simultaneously with this decision, our attention was drawn to various other congregations around the city which were dying and much in need of a transfusion. One in particular was another Evangelical Free Church on the far west side of the city in the potentially explosive, racially changing Austin area. Five years back it had enjoyed a healthy three hundred and fifty attendance but had now dwindled to about thirty people. Having been rejected by the last three pastoral candidates, the people of the Zion church were very close to closing the doors permanently.

We contacted their Board chairman and explained our fears about our numerical growth—we just might have more people than we could handle. Would they be interested in an arrangement whereby we would provide a pastor and some new blood from Circle Church in return for the Zion group's continuing and adapting our program to their building? Their dwindling bank account still had a balance of over $3,000 which could help pay a man's salary.

We seemed to fulfill one another's needs perfectly, and the votes sailed through both congregations. A young man from our congregation, Al Nestor, agreed to take on his first pastoral responsibilities (and in so doing joined our staff at Circle Church), and our people began to pray about whether they should go to Zion church or stay at Circle. The way was led by Board Chairman Bill Weiss and his family.

Another major area began to unfold as we moved into that fall season. Several months after beginning Circle, I had a conversation with the rector of an Episcopal church, several blocks from where we meet. His comments were, "David, if you are able to have a family from the neighborhood attend regularly, you will be accomplishing something I have not been able to do in many, many years."

The first contact we made involved a black family. The father and mother attended a prayer group in the basement of Cook County Hospital's Nursing School at the invitation of a white woman who had been burdened to make calls and work in the neighborhood. On his first visit to Circle Church, Abraham Cuff wasted no time in immediately pinning me with questions as to the purpose of my ministry. Because of his previous church experiences, he was suspicious of my motives; in attempting to clas-

sify the stripe of my clerical cloth, he demanded to know the model
car I drove (a Volkswagen, of course!).

Eventually, Abraham and his family began to attend regularly
and we found their story typical of many. It was the second marriage for both, resulting in five children, two boys and three girls.
A history of spasmodic employment had created financial obligations and aggravated the tendency toward drink. With time, Abraham began to take an interest in our church affairs, leading
discussion groups and eventually becoming a Board member.

One Sunday he related that he had been walking home after
a morning service—he couldn't remember now exactly what had
been preached—when all of a sudden he experienced a clear
understanding of the power and purpose of Christ. Right there on
Jackson Street it was as though a great burden rolled off his back.
In these words, which have great sociological meaning in light of
the position of the Negro male, Abraham expressed his experience
of conversion: "Now I knew for the first time in my life that I
could be the father to my children I had always wanted to be."

It was through many conversations with the Cuff family and the
determined efforts of a young seminarian from Garret Theological
Seminary in Evanston (who left the church eventually because it
wasn't socially concerned enough for him), that I first began to
awake to the staggering needs of the nonstudent portion of our
community. I will never forget taking my little daughter, Melissa,
then three, to visit a family in the neighborhood. She saw some of
her friends from the Sunday school playing ball in a littered empty
lot, jagged with broken bottles. Going up the dark stairway we
were both overwhelmed with the smell of urine in the hall and by
the crude crayon pictures scratched on the walls. The impression
of decay rudely interjected itself into the sheltered womb of her
world, and she began to cry. Often in the despair of it all, I have
had similar feelings.

As time passed, it became apparent to me that a black would
be needed on the staff if we were really to do anything significant.
My background had left me woefully ill-equipped to deal with
these intricately difficult conditions. The first time Karen and I
invited the Cuff family for dinner, we visited Lincoln Park Zoo with
all the kids before returning home together for the meal. Since we

parked the car by the rear courtyard, we naturally went in the back door. I've had no history of being compelled to use back doors because the occupants of homes or businesses considered me to be socially inferior, but Abraham has. It was not until much later that we realized what a social gaff this had been. Fortunately, Abraham entered the front door enough after that to realize we didn't care which entrance he used, only that he came!

I have been stretched and opened since we first began this inner-city phase of our ministry. My contacts with black pastors and social workers and ghetto dwellers have been multiple. Karen privately conducted an intense study on the causes and structure of poverty, but there are still innuendos and implications which are beyond both of us because we have never experienced the humiliations. I have come to the conclusion that there are many things I will never be able to understand because I am not black. I must simply accept them because my black friends say that they are so.

Our congregation was very open to hiring a black man. Because we were so young, much of the prejudice and inhibitions an older group might have demonstrated simply did not exist, or if they did, were being dealt with by the individuals who held them. We wanted an integrated church. That seemed to be one of the distinct advantages of an urban work—the possibility of different races. So Ka Tong, Larry, and I began looking. We talked to several fellows of varying ages and soon began to realize that finding a qualified man, evangelical in his theology, who is truly black in a conceptual sense is not the easiest task in the world. The details were all covered with each applicant—salary, vacations, expenses, etc.—and when each one left, we would all laugh together knowing that though we talked big, there were really no funds to begin with!

It was Larry who came into the office one day and said, "There is a young black in his last year at Moody who is quite militant. His name is Mel Warren, and maybe we ought to talk to him." Mel came for the interview, his hair curling tightly into a natural, and wearing a dashiki. His awareness of the problems of his people had been developed through experience and study. After he shared his experience of finding God while stationed with the Air Force in Spain, he expressed his sincere present desire to serve Christ.

There was no question in our minds but what we had found the person for whom we were looking. The big question was how we were going to underwrite a part-time salary. Our funds were low and some of our regular givers had just transferred to the Zion Church, making it necessary, therefore, to raise the money from outside sources. Again, we began praying and making contacts, and within four weeks the support had been raised. Our congregation approved of Mel. The only static seemed to come from Larry, who wondered if our new staff member would please cooperate and grow some "soul" sideburns!

So before reaching our second birthday, there were five of us on staff—three full-time, two part-time; three whites, one black, one Oriental—myself, Ka Tong Gaw, Larry Mayfield, Al Nestor, and Mel Warren. I had always envisioned the benefits of a team effort. I am wary of the concept which says that God speaks exclusively through one individual whom he chooses. Although I do believe that this happens at times, it seems to me to be fraught with inherent dangers. We all know Christian leaders, over-impressed with their own grandeur, who refuse to submit to the advice and direction of workers holding lesser positions. So enamored of their own individual works are some, that the Spirit of God is no longer with them. It appeared to me that the team concept was a natural safeguard against the insidious power complexes which people in places of authority often experience.

My concept of a team was that of a whole containing equal parts. All of us would be called pastor, with each man having differing areas of responsibility. I once asked a minister with whom I worked if he believed in a team effort. His reply was, "Yes," but I soon discovered that his idea of a team was that of one big chief who set all the policy, made all the decisions, and then ordered all the little chiefs to carry out his desires!

It would be impossible to overestimate the importance of this team concept. It was made possible both by the willingness of our congregation to forgo a building, and by the help of outsiders interested in a city ministry. Let it also be made abundantly clear that the relationships have not been easy. In some ways, our personalities are diametrically opposed to each other. We are very strong individuals who are learning to attain an atmosphere of complete honesty with one another, having established a precedent which allows someone to say, "I disagree."

I learned that a southside Chicago black Christian has very

strong views about Dr. Martin Luther King, Jr., and he is not going to be swayed by my ideas, especially when I admit to ungrounded biases or a lack of reading. I discovered from Ka Tong that a Filipino regards what I term American generosity as American imperialism. We have hassled over such issues as abortion, pacifism (Ka Tong heatedly charged Al once with being a draft dodger, and that evening felt so chagrined he drove to Al's home asking forgiveness), students' rights, eternal security, who is a good Board member, whether to use handclapping in the morning service, salaries—in short, just about everything!

These heated, volatile exchanges could easily have blown us apart, but we learned when to force ourselves to pray, and in those still, precious moments we remember our common cause. A rare camaraderie has formed, and we now all have the courage to be ourselves before one another. We have developed the patience to try to understand and the desire to love and learn. None of us is the same as when we first met. We are all better men for the interaction and will continue to be because that often painful process has not stopped. We have learned that unity in Christ doesn't mean that people have to be identical. It means we can be united in spite of our differences. We have experienced in microcosm what we wish the total congregation could know in this depth.

When Mel first came on the staff, it was often difficult to ascertain his true feelings toward the rest of us. He was vocal on the black issue and how it related to the Christian church or to social concern, but the short time together hadn't given us a personal knowledge of one another. One afternoon Mel returned from a speaking trip out of state. On the plane he had fallen into conversation with his seat companion—what is your job? where do you live?—that sort of thing. The businessman was so moved by Mel's account of his work in the inner city that he extended a hundred dollar bill at the end of the trip. The money was split five ways, and to each of us was given a portion. From that point on we had no more question about Mel. We reasoned that when a Bible school student, whose wife is working to put him through school, shares a windfall of that proportion, he must feel as intensely about you as you do about him!

I am in my middle thirties, but this is my first pastorate. I wonder if I could have endured the strain of this honest relationship five

years later in life. As individual members of a staff we are deliberately choosing to submit ourselves to the authority of the group.
I am extremely grateful the team concept happened at Circle when
it did. Often after our confrontations, Al prays, "Thank you, God,
for the luxury of the staff." One afternoon our district superintendent dropped past the office on a Tuesday, staff day. He was amazed
by the openness and stated that he wished every church staff
could be this same way. He didn't know the half of it! Because of
his presence we were all on particularly good behavior!

Each sermon is now a composite of the thoughts of the five.
Whoever preaches goes over his thoughts with another member
of the team on Monday, or before. If anything basic needs changing, it should come out here. On Tuesday the entire staff hears in
summary the emphasis of the sermon. Again there is criticism and
added perspective from the various backgrounds and viewpoints.
Once or twice more the speaker meets in private session with
other staff members as the week continues. We try to contribute
ideas for illustration or application. We listen carefully for thoughts
which detract from the main thrust rather than enhance it. We
watch for improper English. We attempt to ask how this applies
to Fred, or Jack, or Betty. Will it meet their needs where they are?

On Saturday morning the whole staff has breakfast together,
listens to the sermon, goes over the various parts they will play
in the total service, and then prays. By Sunday morning the material has been well polished and should prove helpful to our
people. The differences of the team have been channeled to become its strengths!

Through the team approach we can relate now to more people.
There are five instead of one for hospital visits, phone calls, counseling, etc. More can speak to us on Sunday after the service, as
well. Once when Ka Tong had preached, my wife heard a voice
behind her comment to a friend, "Would you like to meet Ka Tong?
He is my favorite on the staff." It didn't bother Karen, because this
is as it should be. Some will feel closer to Al, or Larry. Their
personalities will mesh with one another. It is a natural thing and
certainly not a basis for petty jealousies.

I experienced much of this unusual closeness when I was working in Youth for Christ. At that time the emphasis was on training
a "Timothy"—a younger person to take responsibility. Most min-

isters are not anxious for such a relationship because of their own insecurities. As an associate pastor, I found if I did poorly I was a drain, and if I did well, I was a threat. Later, as an assistant pastor, the same was true. A close friend, encouraging me to take a church on my own, said, "An assistant or an associate inherits the same abbreviation on the door." He was right! I vowed never to bind my co-workers by such an arrangement. Now I am learning that the trainer of Timothys has a great learning process to go through as a trainee.

The city is rough on churches, and to go it alone would be very hard. I know many urban pastors, and the great majority are discouraged, defeated, and negative. When I get that way, several of the other fellows are always high, and they seem to draw around the one who needs encouragement. When we all face a problem, we work and pray it out together. It's laughter and hilarity as well as struggle.

So, as of October, 1968, and not yet two years old, we were sitting on top of the world. A team had formed and together we were learning to be strong. The congregation was like a coat of many colors, with people from all parts of the world attending. The spirit was to move ahead. All was on schedule. The association with the Zion church was progressing smoothly. Even some suburbanites were attending and their presence buoyed our congregation. Our relationship with the Teamsters continued to be very good. Publicity (which we had not sought and consequently felt was of God) was beginning to appear about the church in various magazines and periodicals. Our philosophy (which is shared in the following chapter) had solidified, and our methods of implementing it were working well. It looked like we were chiseling a miracle out of the tough concrete of inner-city Chicago.

It all seemed too good to be true, and I began to consider writing a book. One of the members of our church is a well-established author in the Christian field. Jim Hefley predicted, "Dave, I think you'd better put it off awhile. You might be premature."

II.

WHAT IT'S ALL ABOUT

Circle Church
is people—worshiping,
learning, listening,
singing.

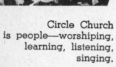

Chapter Three

Why do we have church anyway?

"What is the greatest need of the local church?"

This was the question we struggled with in the months before we started Circle Church—and continued to struggle with as we grew.

The question haunts clergy and laity alike. We of Christendom are achingly aware that something is oppressively wrong with the church, but what? Unfortunately we have established a pattern of grasping at any straw we think will rescue us from the murky grave into which we seem to be sinking. . . ."What the church needs is an aggressive method of person-to-person evangelism." . . . "Seminaries must train men to become thunderous prophets of God.". . ."A vital Christian Education program is the key, because after all the coming generation is the church of the future.". . . "We desperately need people who know the word of God better; therefore we should schedule time for in-depth Bible study."

Helter-skelter we chase after each new cure which might conceivably "save" the church: a practical approach to neighborhood visitation, an outstanding seminary grad who appears to be gifted in working with young people, home cell Bible study groups—all good ideas but none deal with the basic problem.

In our months of discussion and evaluation, what eventually evolved is the philosophy of the church which is given in this chapter. We found that we first had to answer the question "Why does the church exist?" Just as it is foolish to ask whether there is value in using an overhead projector during the morning service if no one has first determined a purpose for that service, so it is equally foolish to become excited about specific solutions to parts of the local church's ministry if a unifying total of what is desired has never been figured out.

This book deals with many new approaches to methodology, but each is rooted in a well-thought-through philosophy of the local church. As far as I am concerned, it is only in the context of how a church functions that value can be assigned to new ideas. Congregations must therefore come to a clear understanding of why they exist before any consideration of methodology be allowed to occur. Only when satisfactory answers are given to such basic questions can patterns be built that are both original and truly helpful.

Conceivably, local churches could be eliminated were it not for the great need Christians have to discuss their faith with one another. An individual believer is able to worship or pray alone, he can share his faith apart from the church, and can even adequately instruct himself along spiritual lines. It is obviously impossible, however, for him to participate in Christian fellowship without others who share his beliefs. I do not mean by this either to deprecate the value of corporate religious activities or to imply that interaction is the most important function of the church. Interaction is, however, that unique need which makes the formation of local church bodies mandatory.

The Church Comes Together

The circle below is the beginning of an all-encompassing diagram that will illustrate our concept of how a church functions. It represents the formation of a congregation from the surrounding society. The need that has precipitated such action is for people to interact around the common interest.

HOW THE LOCAL CHURCH FUNCTIONS

Sociology is the study of group living. It includes the investigation of integrated and nonintegrated groups. The distinguishing
characteristic of a non-integrated group—such as the crowd at a
sporting event—is that members do not meet regularly to communicate with one another about their common interest. In an
integrated group there is sustained interaction regarding some common interest through which the members mutually adjust their
behavior. Well aware that no sociologist would classify the church
as a nonintegrated group, I must admit to a growing fear that more
churches are nonintegrated groups than we care to realize. The
problem is certainly not that the members fail to meet regularly,
but rather that they somehow have misunderstood the importance
of talking about **the common interest** when they do get together!

Apart from the sermons, which are rarely heard or heeded as
well as professional ministers assume, communication is seldom
centered about the Christian faith which is the cohesive element.
Instead, congregations have equated "Christian fellowship" with
potluck suppers, baby showers, Sunday school class socials, and
church picnics—where conversation is about jobs, families, school,
hobbies, sports, romance, and acquaintances, but seldom about
the common faith and its implication for our lives. The peripheral
edges are merely skirted—we mention that the preacher's message
has been a blessing, or whisper that so and so's son is far from the
Lord—but it is with embarrassing difficulty that we bare the condition of our personal spiritual being.

Not only are we unable to expose the treacherous dissents and
agonies of our failures to a loving brotherhood, we cannot even
share the specific ecstasies and triumphs of our faith lest we be
thought super-pious. Our sufferings, therefore, are mute and our
joys are tongue-tied! For the church to qualify as a valid integrated
group, there must be a great adjustment here, with our interaction
beginning to center in our common beliefs and their outworking
in our lives.

Sociologically, the local church is classified as an integrated
group because, supposedly, this effective relating of members to
one another around the common religious tie takes place. I must
continue to maintain that this is exactly where the average congregation is the weakest. Try going up to someone after a morning
service and saying excitedly, "You know, that message was just

for me. In fact, I was reading a fabulous section in Scripture this week that correlates with what the pastor was preaching. Let me find it and read it to you." The chances are that by the time you locate the passage and look up to read it to him, your party is gone. A normal person doesn't talk about the common religious base in church, and he wants to escape such conversations.

In a less threatening situation, however, away from the pulpit and the organ and titles and high ceilings, a layman may feel quite different. Is not the spontaneous growth of home Bible study groups certain testimony to his subconscious recognition of this lack of exchange and to his present desire for readjustment? I do not doubt but what the greater motivation in beginning these small cells across the country, even above evangelism, is the secret craving to discuss one's faith. Multitudes of these small groups forming in homes imply that communication within the church cannot continue to be exclusively equated with hearing a sermon.

And could it be that the immobile pew, backed up in rows, must disappear if congregations are going to interact effectively in the church building? Whatever the answer, it is obvious that the trend is moving away from church people's being satisfied to function exclusively as an audience.

In no age group is the need for interaction more pronounced than among the younger generation who have cut their eye teeth on dialogue in our educational systems. These younger minds can no longer rest secure in the belief that, since the minister felt he had a good grasp of the subject, all was right in God's world. I am told that the bulk of information is so great today that school teachers no longer have sufficient time to cover it all through lecture. Students, therefore, are taught to ask good questions that develop their capacities to achieve learning outside the classroom environment. Unfortunately, when they ask their questions in the church they are suspect. Many older ministers say that the younger generation's problem with the church is that inadequate answers are given to their questions. They feel a greater emphasis must be placed on apologetics. I don't believe this analysis probes deeply enough. The younger mind sees the problem as not being allowed to ask questions to begin with! Opportunity for meaningful discussion is mandatory in this case, or young people will continue to disappear from our ranks.

Never before has this need for interaction been so apparent. We live in a world of alienations—government from government, race from race, generation from generation, husband from wife, father from child and, most poignantly, man from God. These conditions have always existed. Yet, more than any previous generation, our awareness and perception of man's dilemma has been heightened because of the moment-by-moment confrontation with modern technology. Essentially, the message of Christianity is and always has been that man can relate to his God, to his neighbor, and most certainly to his fellow believer. The initial role of the local church, therefore, is to fill this need for valid spiritual interaction as previously defined. When interaction begins, we have an integrated group within society.

Because we recognize our basic need for true spiritual interaction, Circle Church schedules times for sharing about the common tie—our faith. The Service of Interaction at 10:45 each Sunday is an example of a meeting specifically designed to fulfill this purpose. Since a more detailed explanation is given later in the book as to how, through methodology, we accomplish our philosophy, it will only be necessary to state here that interaction has been the key to the effective mixing of the various racial, economic, educational, cultural, and age differences within the congregation.

Nothing is more demanding than attempting to preach to the diversity of needs represented in the average urban church. But miraculously, as people talk in small groups about what the Bible teaches and how to apply these truths, meaningful fellowship occurs and the artificial barriers disappear. No matter how much one desires it, it is difficult to love somebody you don't know. Conversely, it is difficult not to love someone you have learned to understand regardless of the differences.

Once sharing began at Circle Church, it was as though the dike had been unplugged. Our dinner table became a constant forum on current religious topics. People lingered after church services continuing discussions on humility, or the Christian and violence, or Christ's teaching on forgiveness. There began to be an exchange of Christian literature, both classical and current. The congregation became so enamored with Christian interaction that at times it would have been a welcome relief to have returned to a normal conversation about baseball, or business, or even babies!

The initial role of the local church is to fill the need for true spiritual interaction.

INTERACTION

HOW THE LOCAL CHURCH FUNCTIONS

The Church Speaks to God

It has been established that interaction is the original need precipitating the formation of a local church. The next question which must be answered is, "How, then, does the corporate body speak to God?" The answer is, at least in part, that the church speaks to God through worship. But probably no more ambiguous word can be found in all of the terminology of the traditional church than the word "worship." What is worship? Most people have a hazy concept, but have never taken time to pin it down!

While serving as President of the Evangelical Ministers' Association of Greater Chicago, I programmed one entire meeting for the pastors to work on defining the term. After discussion by small groups and a pooling of the results, the men concluded that worship was anything a Christian does as long as it is done in an attitude of wanting to please God. This definition could possibly be valid if worship is thought of in a very broad sense, but it also produces a serious difficulty. The definition is so general that there is hardly any way one can work with it when it comes to incorporating worship into a service. Anything becomes worship as long as the desire to please God is present when one acts. But is there not a difference between singing "Holy, holy, holy, Lord God almighty" and "Rescue the perishing"?

According to Webster, to worship is to attribute worth to deity. If I say I appreciate my fellow staff members because they are honest, hardworking, etc., I am attributing worth to them. When I transfer my attention vertically to God and tell Him the value I place on Him because of who He is, I am attributing worth to God, or worshiping.

For example: "God, I praise You because You are Spirit. You don't have bodily parts that deteriorate with age, nor are you

limited by physical exhaustion. Because of this, You will function
eternally at the peak of efficiency. You do not have to sleep because of weariness, so at any time I can instantly have your attention. I appreciate this about You."

The Old Testament writers were extremely proficient at attributing worth to God. They diligently practiced the art of worshiping
and I am sure their entire concept of God was vastly expanded as
a result. How often the twentieth-century mind looks at that ancient
Judaic heritage with false superiority. "Their concept of the Godhead was not as developed as ours is today," we self-righteously
exclaim. Yet most Christians are barely able to offer rudimentary
private prayers of praise, much less to participate in worship on a
congregational level.

One morning during our first year of operation, a young student
agreed to give the invocation. I carefully explained that it was to
be exclusively in the area of praise. He came a half-hour early on
Sunday morning pleading for help because he couldn't think of
anything to say! Because as a staff we have exerted such effort at
Circle Church to instruct our congregation as to what worship truly
is and to lead them in creative forms of it, such an incident among
us today would be very uncommon.

**The local church speaks to God through corporate worship and
prayer.**

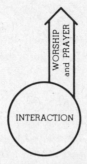

HOW THE LOCAL CHURCH FUNCTIONS

The two words, worship and prayer, are not synonymous, although they do have many parallels. As we have previously

defined it, worship is basically the praise and adoration of God. It is not necessarily **just** prayer, because it can be expressed in a variety of forms such as music, Scripture reading, the giving of offerings, liturgies, art forms, celebrations. David's dance before the Lord may have been a celebration, or it may have been an example of one of those spontaneous expressions of praise which have no articulated form but which are worship also. Prayer is speaking to God, but it is not necessarily all worship. It can include adoration and praise. But whenever prayer moves into the area of request, it ceases to be an act of worship. Again, when we use the word worship, it means to attribute worth to deity.

Our Service of Worship and Instruction is at 9:30 on Sunday morning. Instruction is included in this title because the hour is not totally worship. For example, whenever a sermon is introduced, specific adoration and praise of God are precluded, and the congregation enters into a time of corporate instruction when God is speaking to them.

I am strongly of the opinion that most churches would aid their congregations if they would call their services, "The Service of Worship, Announcements, Etc." At least it would indicate they knew there was a difference! Any process of semantics can become exhaustively mundane, but this examination of terms is necessary if the modern church is to eliminate the foggy concepts which are rendering her impotent to determine her purpose.

Our Service of Worship and Instruction is generally divided into three sections:

The Approach to God in Worship.

God Speaking Through His Written Word.

The Response of Obedience.

Congregational worship is the exclusive objective of the first section. Music in the approach to God always expresses adoration, praise, or possibly thanksgiving, whether it is a congregational hymn, a choral selection, or a special musical number. The choices are not based so much on the style of music as on the text—are the words addressed to God and do they speak of His worth? The prayer or invocation is never general but centers on God's attributes. Any reading of Scripture in this portion of the service, whether from the platform or responsively, in unison or silently, will always be addressed to God. We are continually discovering that worship

does not have to be heavy or pompous or dull. Quite the opposite.
Some of the most exciting moments in the church are when we
have figured out ways to praise God corporately that He is Light,
or creative, or everywhere present.

We have found that once the meaning of worship is understood,
it is possible as a congregation to praise God without comfortably
padded pews or maroon carpets, without elegant chandeliers or
vaulted ceilings. A massive sign advertises "Teamsters' Union
Hall—Local No. 705" from the front wall. A hardwood dance floor
amplifies the footsteps of latecomers. The elevated train often
manages to rumble past during a scheduled time of silent meditation, and we have constant competition from the police and
ambulance sirens which rush through the calamitous community.
The lobby telephone can ring or the janitor's bell sound at any
unexpected moment. Yet, in the midst of this, Sunday by Sunday
we are truly worshiping God together.

We have established that the local church speaks to God through
worship and prayer. Although prayer is included in the morning
services, it is emphasized in the services of prayer throughout the
week. These are conducted once or twice a month per geographic
area in small home groups. We discovered that there were not
enough church-wide prayer requests to merit our meeting each
week as a total body. There are many personal requests, however,
and these are shared in an intimate and trusting way because of
the closeness which develops in small groups. In order to protect
these cells from becoming inclusive, all-church prayer meetings
are scheduled every so often on a Sunday night. Anyone is welcome to attend any of the prayer groups, or all of them, if they
desire. And several do.

In previous church midweek prayer meetings, we had noticed
that the lack of specific requests was usually overlooked because
the time was filled by more sermonizing. It seemed foolish to us to
spend a large block of the evening listening to another lecture in
the service of prayer, when there was such a need in our lives
for an unhurried period to share personal requests with one another. The requests that had come in traditional surroundings were
boringly repetitious, centering mainly around beds of sickness,
unsaved relatives, and missionaries around the world. If you have
been to one such meeting, you've been to them all!

It is Circle Church's philosophy to have one or two groups meeting during a midweek night; the congregation is encouraged to attend monthly a specific one in their geographic area. We are excited about the worship service and the discussion groups, but somehow the small prayer cells are the most rewarding of all. The intense personal honesty which is displayed in them is a new and refreshing experience to me.

God Speaks to the Church

The initial role of the local church is to fill the need for Christian fellowship. The local church speaks to God through corporate worship and prayer. But how does God speak to the local congregation? We know that God speaks to individuals through circumstances, but if He used this method to speak to the corporate body, each member would interpret the circumstances differently and would probably end up in a fight. God speaks through Scripture. But He can do so through an individual's private reading. Is there a need for believers to form a corporate body in order to engage in private Bible reading? How does God speak to the local church? At Circle we struggled to find an all-encompassing category. After a year of continued discussions, we began to discover that God speaks to the local church by means of the gifts of the Holy Spirit.

God speaks to . . . the local church by means of the gifts of the Holy Spirit.

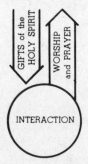

HOW THE LOCAL CHURCH FUNCTIONS

The action does not stop here. God speaks not only to the corporate body as it is assembled, but to the individual members of the body who minister to one another, and eventually to those outside the church through the same method. God speaks to, **and through,** the local church by means of the gifts of the Holy Spirit. The total exciting diagram looks like this:

God speaks to, and through, the local church by means of the gifts of the Holy Spirit.

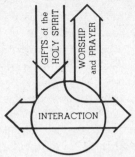

HOW THE LOCAL CHURCH FUNCTIONS

We have too long avoided the specifics of the ministry of the Holy Spirit. We have dwelt on the fringe and majored in generalities. We all know that Christians are supposed to be "filled with" the Spirit, but our vague understanding has left us with an important frustration. Most Christians live with defeat because they have not realized that at conversion the Holy Spirit comes to live within them. It is no wonder that the powerful impact of this truth has been overlooked, since in so few of our evangelistic efforts is the ministry of the Holy Spirit adequately emphasized. I continually hear messages on conversion where the Holy Spirit is not even mentioned! This preaching implies that God is interested only in forgiving the past so that the convert is fit for Heaven, while the present and the future are left in his own insufficient human hands. I have heard it said from pulpits that the single reason God allows us to remain on earth is to help other people experience the same awareness of forgiveness and assurance of eternity. This is a great perversion! Does God have no desire that man now experience, in and through his own spirit, life that is truly filled with meaning and beauty?

As a youngster I can remember listening avidly to the Lone Ranger series over the radio. The program invariably ended with someone asking, to the accompaniment of distantly fading hoofbeats, "Who is that masked rider, anyway?" My response to that question was always an incredulous "How could anyone not know? After all, how many men disguised by a black mask ride a great white stallion, shoot silver bullets, and travel with a faithful Indian companion?" The same response rises within me now when I see the ignorance behind so many questions about the person of the Holy Spirit. His work and characteristics are so obvious in Scripture, how is it that we don't know who He is?

While I was writing these pages, a young man wandered into our offices. Disheveled and dirty, he had been mercilessly beaten the night before by an acquaintance, and his face was an assortment of welts and bruises. After a period of conversation I felt that he was not posturing for a handout, but had truly reached the point of no exit. Someone had told him that the people at Circle Church were Christians, and he was grabbing feebly for some faint straw of hope.

As his story unfolded—abandonment by parents, a history of street affairs, alcoholism—I responded with the message of a relationship to God in Christ Jesus. Carefully I explained the role of the Holy Spirit and made a point of remarking that God was willing now to make his body, as misused and neglected as it had become, a home for His Spirit. We then shared in one of those thrilling moments of conversion when a man casts himself upon the mercies of his Creator and knows without hesitation that an encounter has occurred.

A job was located along with temporary housing. In an effort not to abandon this young man to a shaky future alone, the staff welcomed him to shadow us as we carried out our various responsibilities. In one of these moments he confided this thought, which is such a pathetic thermometer of our problem: "You know, I had always heard that God wanted to forgive my sins and save me from hell, but no one ever told me about the Holy Spirit and how He can empower an individual to live a meaningful life."

A friend in her fifties recently commented that years ago it was natural to assume that when a man made an initial commitment to Christ, miracles would happen. He would be delivered from drink, broken relationships would be restored, personal affairs would untangle. "We expected these things to happen naturally at conversion," she pondered, "and they did." I wonder if we have so intellectualized our theology that we can no longer believe. Maybe we have become too desensitized to care. At any rate, in eliminating the activity of God's Spirit in the message we proclaim, we have stripped the message of its power. Have we forgotten that an essential truth of Christianity is that we no longer need to live with defeat? Have we forgotten that the Christian is supposed to be different in power from the world around him? Do so many of us no longer believe in the miraculous change of a life style that we have hindered its occurrence?

Not only did God forgive us the ills that blocked us from Him, He imparted His Spirit to dwell within us to help us. So much is this the case that Paul calls our bodies "temples of the Holy Spirit." Through this indwelling, each of us has also been given a gift or gifts by the Holy Spirit with which to serve Christ as a part of His church. These gifts must now be explained clearly before returning to the discussion of how God speaks to and through the church.

The Gifts of the Spirit

In the twelfth chapter of Romans, Paul writes, "Having gifts that differ according to the grace given to us, let us use them: if prophecy, in proportion to our faith; if service, in our serving; he who teaches, in his teaching; he who exhorts, in his exhortation; he who contributes, in liberality; he who gives aid, with zeal; he who does acts of mercy, with cheerfulness." Prophecy, serving, teaching, exhorting, contributing, giving aid, and doing acts of mercy all are listed as gifts of the Holy Spirit. In 1 Corinthians 12, verses 8 to 10, additional illustrations are shared by the same writer:

> To one is given through the Spirit the utterance of wisdom, and to another the utterance of knowledge according to the same Spirit, to another faith by the same Spirit, to another gifts of healing by the one Spirit, to another the

working of miracles, to another prophecy, to another the
ability to distinguish between spirits, to another various
kinds of tongues, to another the interpretation of tongues.

The word "illustrations" is used purposely, because I do not believe Paul anywhere intends to give an exhaustive list of the gifts.

In the fourth chapter of Ephesians, in a paragraph that centers on
gifts of the various roles of the ministry, Paul introduces still more
examples. If an all-inclusive catalog of gifts had been intended, I
believe these passages would contain identical listings, especially
since they are written by the same author. Just as I believe the
various aspects of the fruit of the Spirit as identified in Galatians 5
(love, joy, peace, etc.) are representative—that is, the writer does
not intend to include every possible virtuous quality—so the
scriptural gifts of the Holy Spirit are to be understood in a similar
way. Therefore, it seems obvious to me that there are gifts not
included in the New Testament listings, such as music, writing,
painting, dramatics, etc.

A casual analysis of the various samples of gifts of the Holy
Spirit found in Scripture seems to show that some are supernatural
and others are not. Would it not require beyond-normal human
capabilities to perform a miracle, accomplish a non-medical healing, or speak in an unknown tongue? On the other hand, what
special touch from God is needed to teach, contribute, or give aid?
To correct the error of this type of thinking, let it be stated emphatically that **all** the gifts of the Holy Spirit are supernatural!

From this point on in the discussion I will not talk about the gifts
of the Holy Spirit where it is obvious one needs an extra touch
from God in order to accomplish them (such as miracles or heal-
ings). I will center my thoughts on those gifts it would appear we
can accomplish on our own without any supernatural aid, such as
teaching or doing acts of mercy. The key to the outworking of
these "human" abilities beyond our own natural capabilities is
found in the individual's attitude toward them. An experience
from my personal life can illustrate this.

In the early days of my ministry, composing a sermon was only
slightly less than traumatic because of my zeal to excel and the
natural conflicts this presented. I was aware of an innate talent for
public speaking and wanted to use this talent for God; but I was

continually dissatisfied with the effectiveness of my efforts—I longed for a greater sense of the supernatural. As I had more opportunity to preach and was forced to spend more time in Scripture, I unearthed verses that dealt with the gifts of the Holy Spirit and began praying earnestly for the gift of prophecy or of teaching. Often, while working on a message, I would sense a real need for help. I would again voice my request to God, but nothing special happened and I was regularly disappointed. Because assurance of my conversion had come in a dramatic way, I expected the gift to arrive similarly. I fully believed that sometime as I prayed I would receive a special "sensation" from God that would assure me my prayer was answered.

The conclusion of my preparation always found a desk piled with books and disarrayed sheets of notes and clippings. Attempting to organize the disorder, I would review the basic contents. Once while doing so I discovered a scrawled thought that was exciting and pertinent. In order to document it, I searched for the source and only after an extended period abandoned the effort.

Continuing my prayers in the following weeks I gradually became aware of the recurrence of more and more thoughts that came from "nowhere." They were always the best ideas—a concise statement of the principles I had been agonizing to express; a life application that would bring me, the preacher, on my knees before God; a sentence that would summarize the total effort and give me a handle with which to work. Then I began to understand! God was answering my prayer, not in an experience of flashing lights or tingling sensations, but in the routine course of sermon preparation. My hand was writing what His Spirit was impressing on my mind as I studied the Scripture. He was quietly guiding my thoughts. When Sundays came I was ready to preach with a new confidence.

Peter speaks about this secret in his first letter when he states, "As each has received a gift, employ it for one another . . . : whoever speaks, as one who utters oracles of God" (4:10-11). The oracles were to be God's, not other men's thoughts, as good as they might be. Gradually, that massive section of my library, the sermon books and commentaries, began to decrease as unworthy volumes were discarded, and only a few came to replace them. Now I spend the greatest part of sermon preparation time with my Bible, a textual commentary to insure accuracy, and in prayer. I feel very confident that I am a person who is speaking God's words, and since the message is first vital to me, it is very likely it will be to my congregation as well.

This problem is far from a magic formula. I am sure I work harder in sermon preparation now than before, but I am also very aware of supernatural guidance. I no longer need human critics to insure the validity of what I preach. I know I have delivered what God desires, because the very preparation has been fresh and challenging. It must be added that the gifts of the Holy Spirit are intricately interwoven with the fabric of one's spiritual well-being. I am sharply aware that my life and attitude of commitment must be pure before God if I am to have effective use of this sacred conferment.

Let me repeat once again to be certain I am understood. In those areas where I have natural abilities, such as a facility for public speaking, the difference between their being talents or gifts of the Holy Spirit is found in my attitude. If I recognize the talent as from God, and in prayer and continual dedication commit it to Him to be used in ministry in a special way, it becomes a gift of the Holy Spirit with supernatural expression. The proof of this is seen in the gradual way God increases this gift for His service. "For His service" is an important phrase, because talents not used in ministry cannot be considered potential gifts. (1 Cor. 12:7: "To each is given the manifestation of the Spirit **for the common good."**) Gifts are given for the exclusive use of ministry!

In the sentence quoted about speaking oracles, Peter does not refer exclusively to the professional clergy. Including, by illustration, other members of the church, he finishes his sentence with the words, "Whoever renders service, as one who renders it by the strength which God supplies." Here is the same principle in operation. If I am given the ability by God to render service, I commit that ability to God and ask Him to use it in a special way. In that act it becomes a gift of the Holy Spirit. I then render service "through the strength which God supplies"!

In this same paragraph in 1 Peter 4, and again in Romans 12, we are instructed to practice hospitality ungrudgingly toward one another. When a woman realizes that, like preaching, hospitality can be a gift of the Holy Spirit, her kitchen can be transformed from a place of drudgery to the nerve center of her ministry. Before, she entertained because no one else would, or because as a Christian she felt obligated. Now she recognizes this opportunity as having come from God and in prayer tells Him of her desire to use this talent in ministry. Soon she begins to notice the natural joy that expresses itself when our gifts are functioning. There is added strength. Her home becomes a place where conversations center about Christ naturally, without contrivance. Her living room serves part-time as a chapel; her dining table is a place of communion; and, according to Scripture, she may even entertain angels! She is aware of the difference between a facility for entertaining and a gift of hospitality!

All the gifts of the Spirit, then, are supernatural, and the illustrations are limitless. The difference between a talent and a gift of the Holy Spirit is found in my attitude. Do I in recognizing my talents see a need beyond my own abilities, and do I then regularly commit these specific abilities to God? If so, I will in practice soon begin to see the distinction.

Like Paul, a man may have more than one gift; consequently he bears more responsibility. **But all in the church have a minimum of one gift.** 1 Peter 4:10: "As each has received a gift"; Ephesians 4:7: "But grace was given to each of us according to the measure of Christ's gift"; 1 Corinthians 12:7: "To each is given the manifestation of the Spirit for the common good." Every true member of the local church has a minimum of one gift, and most people have many. Since no one has every gift, and everyone has at least one, there exists an interdependence among the members of the church. Scripture teaches (1 Cor. 12:22-25) that the less spectacular gifts are more necessary than the showy ones. In other words, the church can go a long time without a miracle, but let it try to exist without acts of mercy or contributions! Yet, if any part of me ceases to function, the total me experiences pain or limitations in some way. How disabled the body of Christ has become because our primary purpose for church attendance has been to hear one man exercise his gifts, rather than to prepare all the people to develop their gifts for ministry, not only within the church but also to society.

This approach toward gifts is indicated in the attitude of church staffs toward their congregations. In so many instances, the clergy begin with a program and then ask, "How can we get our people to fit into it?" At Circle we begin with our people and ask, "What gifts do they have? How can we help our people use these gifts in ministry either inside or outside the structure of Circle Church?" Here is an immense difference! The gifts of the people determine our program. We don't want to moan pleadingly, "If we had twenty more neighborhood tutors, we could fill our quota." We start with the gifts of the people. Perhaps there are thirty who feel they have a gift of teaching and would like to meet this special need of deprived neighborhood children. They then **are** the quota. Only then do we make the neighborhood contacts. The program must never control the people!

If we do not have people who are specifically gifted to meet the needs of a given program, then we drop the program. This would be true even in areas that are considered very important in the church. Let it be stated strongly, however, that we believe the Holy Spirit to be perfectly adept at distributing gifts properly among the people of the congregation, and the **important** areas of ministry are automatically taken care of through His divine foresight.

Occasionally, a member will notify you that he believes he has a gift about which you have serious misgivings. How well I remember Abraham, our first convert from the neighborhood, saying, "So much has been done for me by the people of this church that now I want to do something for somebody, too."

"What is it you want to do?" I asked.

"Preach," came the definite reply.

Now even the staff faces our much-degreed student congregation with a dose of hesitancy. But I recognized that this black man's appeal had validity. It is hard to be continually on the receiving end. So we scheduled him to preach on a Sunday evening. Abraham did surprisingly well for a man with no training and little formal education. The experience only whetted his appetite and he was back again soon, very soon, wanting more of the same.

Three men were invited to share the preaching time one Sunday morning, and among them was Abraham. The other two were well-educated and had years of Bible study behind them. I spent several sessions with Abraham helping him prepare for his eight minutes.

When the morning arrived he appeared very nervous, and I soon realized he had been drinking. I began then to doubt the wisdom of this venture. (It should be stated parenthetically that drinking is far more tolerated by the poor people in the inner city than by the accepted white suburban Christian standard.) You can imagine my surprise when he presented a sermon clear and moving, beautiful in its simplicity. It was short, but it had great feeling. He clearly did have a gift which the Lord could use.

I complimented him after the service. "Oh, Pastor David," he said, "I was so nervous about getting up in front of all those people and talking that I just had to have something to help me. But, you know, I think I can do it next time without the nip."

God Speaks To and Through the Local Church

It is by means of these gifts of the Holy Spirit that God speaks to and through the local church. He speaks **to** the assembled body, represented by the circle, through gifts of the Holy Spirit such as preaching, teaching, music, and dramatics.

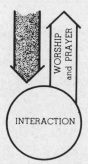

HOW THE LOCAL CHURCH FUNCTIONS

In the staff at Circle Church we have a growing fear of any sin in our lives that would cause us to mouth our own words, not those of God, to the congregation. The hollow sermon is never ended soon enough for one who has spoken oracles! Many of the musicians have expressed this same dread. They do not want to sing any longer simply in their own strength. There have even been those who have refused to read Scripture during a service because their lives were not exemplary of the truths proclaimed in that particular passage.

God speaks **through** the gifts of the Holy Spirit as members of the local church mutually minister to one another through acts of mercy, wisdom, service, giving aid, etc.

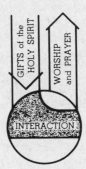

HOW THE LOCAL CHURCH FUNCTIONS

Because Circle Church had an unusually young congregation, we were not as proficient with the business of incorporation and finances as a more experienced group would have been. After hobbling along for months, these affairs were finally taken in hand by a newer arrival, who soon had the administrative areas functioning smoothly and who transformed our financial tangles into a machine humming with proficiency.

Upon thanking him profusely for his willing assistance, I was taken aback when he looked me straight in the eye and replied, "Don't thank me. I'm just doing my part in the body through the gifts God has given me." When the people in your congregation start preaching your sermons back to you, you know your message is getting across.

Another illustration of how people within the body minister to one another through the gifts of the Holy Spirit and how the purposes of the local church are intertwined will prove helpful at this point.

Largely through the experience of interacting, Circle Church stumbled on the fact that it is virtually impossible for sensitive Christians to hear a brother articulating a need without trying to fill that need. Having confessed in an interaction group one Sunday morning that the biggest obstacle she faced toward establishing regular devotions was the responsibilities of being a wife and mother, one woman was overwhelmed when her doorbell rang three times that week with separate offers from three individuals to help wash down the cupboards, mend clothes, and iron laundry. Without the interaction none would have known her need, but when the need was shared, body ministry began to occur spontaneously throughout the congregation. These ladies were ministering as certainly with their gifts as I do with mine.

God also speaks through the church to the outside world by means of the gifts of the Holy Spirit.

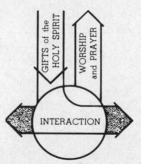

HOW THE LOCAL CHURCH FUNCTIONS

The natural gift to illustrate this concept is witnessing. For a long time I felt it imperative that we all speak to others about Christ. But now I believe that not everyone in the body has this specific gift. In fact, some Christian leaders have taken this difficult gift and tried to equate it solely with outreach. Is evangelism limited to "witnessing"? What about acts of mercy, giving aid, hospitality? I believe there are many groups who will never be reached by our usual evangelistic efforts until some of the other gifts are exercised first. I am thinking of the hostility many blacks feel toward white culture, which even extends to what they have termed the "white Jesus." It has been our experience at Circle that the simple gift of hospitality had to be extended to the people of our neighborhood before we ever had opportunity to exercise that more difficult gift—verbalizing our faith.

This concept of the church ministering through each member as he is empowered by the Holy Spirit greatly alters the role of the pastor. In his book "Company of the Committed," Elton Trueblood compares the minister's position to that of a coach in charge of helping each player develop to the fullest of his potential for the sake of the team. In Ephesians 4:11-12, a comma, which many scholars agree should never have been added, clouds the meaning of an important passage. It should read, "And his gifts were that some should be . . . pastors and teachers, for the equipment of the saints [no comma] for the work of ministry." The Episcopalian, Sam Shoemaker, defined the role of the pastor even more specifically as the playing coach, someone who, while trying to bring out the best in others, coaches from the hub of activity. He is extremely important, but he doesn't do all the running and blocking and passing and play-calling.

When this philosophy and its implications are understood, we see the local church operating with the kind of precision maneuvers of a modern football team, where each man is alive to his exact function, yet there is great opportunity for spontaneity. If someone is sick in the church, there is no need to inform the chairman of the hospital visitation committee. Each member, aware of his unique gifts, knows when he should move to carry out his role. The same is true when an appeal is made for teachers, finances, flowers, etc. As we move forward in this attitude, all those feelings so common to us before—"Do I have to?" "I did it last year" "Get someone else"—begin to disappear. The man whose giving has for years kept the church solvent does not despair that he has led no one to the Lord, if this is not his gift. Nor does he begrudge being told of a financial need if contributing is one of his major roles.

It is now no longer enough for me, as a pastor, to feel satisfied with a solitary display of my gift. My ministry must include assisting each one in our congregation to find expression for his particular gift or gifts, either within the framework of the organized church or beyond it. My prayer time exemplifies this new attitude; my requests regarding members include a desire for wisdom to help each discover his spiritual potential and possible areas of service. Some need no help. Others, so accustomed to pew-sitting, present a great challenge.

The Church at Work

Acts 2:42-47 is a wonderful illustration of the principles this book has discussed so far. **The initial role of the local church is to fill the need for Christian fellowship.** "And they devoted themselves to . . . fellowship" (v. 42).

HOW THE LOCAL CHURCH FUNCTIONS

The local church speaks to God through corporate worship and prayer. "And they devoted themselves to . . . the breaking of bread and the prayers . . . praising God" (vv. 42, 47).

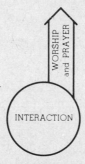

HOW THE LOCAL CHURCH FUNCTIONS

God speaks to and through the local church by means of the gifts of the Holy Spirit. "And they devoted themselves to the apostles' teaching . . . and many wonders and signs were done through the apostles. And all who believed were together and had all things in common; and they sold their possessions and goods and distributed them to all, as any had need. . . . And the Lord added to their number day by day those who were being saved" (vv. 42-45, 47).

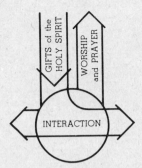

HOW THE LOCAL CHURCH FUNCTIONS

From our point of view it is not adequate to say that the job of the local church is to build up the saints and evangelize the world. This answer is much too simplistic. That is why I have spent considerable time developing these points and repeating the chart, because once these thoughts are clearly understood, some very logical implications follow. One of the reasons it is so difficult to implement any new ideas from the exciting multitude which are beginning to explode everywhere is that we have no basic philosophy of operation from which to work. Consequently, the new ideas, which are excellent in their own right, serve only to confuse our already disoriented outlook. We major on parts rather than attempting to look at the whole of the problem.

It is easy to see why the local church is experiencing difficulties. Does the normal congregation carry on meaningful interaction? The answer is usually no! The prayer and worship are seldom inspiring or significant, and the gifts of the Holy Spirit are avoided like the plague. If what I have shared is truly the way a local church should function, then it is no wonder our problems are of an immense nature.

Chapter Four

"I was glad when they said unto me..."

Visiting Circle Church for the first time, you would be immediately aware of obvious physical differences from the usual church sanctuary—hundreds of folding chairs arranged semicircular fashion, each with an ash tray fastened on the back; little boys intently putting hymnals on every other seat; the Teamsters' insignia squarely centered above the front platform; a long table holding a metal lectern substituting for a pulpit; a jumble of wires leading to microphones, tape recorders, and a slide or overhead projector; a movie screen serving as backdrop for it all.

As the hall filled, you would be unable to ignore the variations of skin color. You might take special note of the mixed couples—black/white, Oriental/Latin American—certainly of the racial composition of the staff as they take their place on the one-step platform.

If you are used to a traditional church, the predominantly youthful look of the congregation would surprise you (as well as the unusual proportion of expectant mothers!). The wild assortment of styles—maxi skirts and minis, jeans and striped bell bottoms, pant suits, saris, African caftans, beards (and bald heads)—would not go unnoticed. Maybe with some relief you would observe that the "straights" are amply represented. A young man with long hair and sandals passes; you might be even more surprised by his presence if you knew that he had been accepted by Wycliffe Bible Translators for translation work. Looking around, you probably would agree with some of our young men who claim that the prettiest girls in the city come to Circle Church.

Suddenly the choir begins to sing a cappella from the rear of the

71

SERVICE OF WORSHIP AND INSTRUCTION

Selected Reading
Prelude

The Approach to God in Worship
(God is Light)

Call to Worship
Hymn 4—"Light of the World, We Hail Thee"
Musical Selection
Invocation
Choral Selection

God Speaking Through His Written Word

Sermon
Multiple Scripture Reading
Choral Selection

The Response of Obedience

Question
Silent Meditation
Musical Selection
Suggestions for Life Response
Hymn 84—"Lo! He Comes"
Offering and Offertory
Choral Response

auditorium. As the service continues it may be strictly offbeat
—something unlike anything you have experienced in your years
of attending church. Or, depending on the Sunday, it could be
more traditional in form, with the sermon an emphatic plea for a
greater Christian social consciousness. From the moment of the
prelude to the last chord following the benediction, however, you
would probably be aware that a single basic theme had been
expressed. You might also conclude there had been a plan behind
the entire hour; it hadn't simply "happened."

Continuing to analyze the morning's service you would have
noticed the attempt at honesty which was displayed in various
interactions. It might have been the staff members in a programmed
time for spontaneous dialogue regarding the content of the sermon,
or the candor of a pastor in fielding questions from the congregation, or the members in reaction to one another during a discussion
group in the hour following the service. In whatever form, its presence could have not been denied. As you attended more often, you
would discover that each Sunday is a weekly implementation of
the philosophy of Circle Church which has been discussed in the
preceding chapter.

Planning the Service

The purpose behind the services down to each individual part is
not left to chance. Exactly the opposite is true. At the conclusion of
the service one morning, a woman visiting from another congregation said to me, "My dear David, how God Himself must have been
here today! The way the Holy Spirit in His own manner put all the
ingredients together was just phenomenal!"

I appreciated her comment, because the Holy Spirit **had** put the
services together, but not quite in the way she intimated—that of a
great gluing force acting mystically and existentially. The Holy
Spirit had motivated our thoughts as we agonized the week and
sometimes weeks before to form our purpose sentence. He had
wooed and we had yielded to His prodding at the personal needs
in our lives during sermon preparation. He had creatively inspired
as we thumbed through hymnals for appropriate music. He had
been in the service. But no, He was not haphazard.

Actually, the planning for any service begins almost a half year before it occurs, when we designate specific preaching assignments in advance. Broad general themes are chosen after regular evaluations by the staff as to the direction in which the church is headed. These emphases are checked against a yearly criteria which requires that the pulpit ministry relate continually to the Old Testament, the Gospels, and the Epistles. If our study of the church calendar indicates that one of these areas has been neglected, we are careful to emphasize it in the proper course of time. Specific preaching themes arise from staff discussion which investigates current church needs. We try to build around a given theme for a number of months until we feel that the congregation has been saturated with it. Then we move on.

We have found that it is good to maintain one sustaining voice that interweaves itself through the fabric of the year. Consequently, I normally preach three Sundays out of five with the other staff sharing the rest. Not only would the congregation be overexposed to me if I preached every Sunday, but I insist that the traditional role of the pastor which demands that he speak three times a week is ridiculous. If we were forced to watch the same TV program three times a week, week after week, year after year, its content consisting of nothing but lecture, our interest would soon pale. The same principle applies to the pulpit. In addition, I am skeptical as to whether any man has enough time in one week to prepare adequately three sermons, each of which is pertinent or inspirational. We have one preaching service a week, and it is not unusual for a Circle minister to spend twenty hours of the preceding week in sermon preparation.

Perhaps many of these theories grew out of experiences which we faced during our first year in the Pastor's Class which follows the 9:30 morning service and is for anyone who wants to talk further about the sermon. I used to initiate the discussion by asking, "Would someone here tell me what you think I was trying to say in the last hour?" The response was most discouraging because seldom did anyone get the intended emphasis correct. Two possible explanations for this existed. First, we were poor preachers. (We vehemently decried this suggestion!) Second, the people had not developed a habit of listening closely. (The truth probably lay somewhere between the two choices.)

Whatever the reason, the solution seemed to be in establishing a basic thrust to our message. Now, whoever preaches must capsulate his sermon into a basic purpose sentence. Without that sentence we cannot form a service. When the sentence has been finalized (by Tuesday, staff day, for the following Sunday), the entire service is developed thematically to enhance that truth.

This is a difficult discipline to establish, but a most important one. Because once we started to do this, almost immediately we found that the congregation was understanding our messages! In fact, the staff often accuses me of repeating the purpose sentence too much. They may be right, but I find it immensely satisfying when a member of the congregation repeats in total the thrust of a message which was preached months or years before. And this happens frequently! If we can establish one basic truth per week, I feel we are accomplishing a tremendous amount.

To assist our congregation further, whoever preaches tries to have an assignment printed in the bulletin on the preceding Sunday. It may be selected Scripture to read at home, or a mental exercise such as thinking through the difference between happiness and joy. It may involve discussing with a friend certain attitudes toward revenge. One example of a bulletin assignment is:

> Next Sunday Pastor Mains will preach from 1 Peter 5:8, 9 on what to do in the teeth of temptation. What temptation most repeatedly troubles you? As you face it this coming week, analyze and list the efforts you make to overcome it.

Often during the week someone will call the church office asking what the assignment was, as they were unable to attend on Sunday. In all I would estimate that about one-fourth of the people actually do what is requested—not as many as we would like, but 25 percent more than would usually be prepared if no assignment had been given.

I have already described the process by which the whole staff helps to prepare the sermon (see Chapter Two). As far as the service is concerned, two jobs remain prior to the Tuesday staff meeting—to pick a fitting bulletin cover from the undated supply on hand, and to decide what attribute or characteristic of God best matches the purpose and emphasis of the sermon. When the staff is all together on Tuesday, we analyze the previous week's service, examining carefully the integral whole, critiquing the sermon, stating what we felt was meaningful and what was not and why. Then we begin to build the service for the following Sunday. The purpose sentence of the sermon is shared along with the general direction the sermon is to take. We discuss whether the attribute of God which has been chosen is consistent with the theme which is to be preached. In our Saturday meeting we check final assignments for the service, as well as listen to the sermon.

Before developing any further the exciting discoveries we have experienced in worship, it will be important to reiterate one point and to emphasize another. First, we have clearly defined worship as attributing worth to God. Second, we have chosen a general three-part pattern for the morning service: The Approach to God in Worship, God Speaking Through His Written Word, and The Response of Obedience. **But we are not inflexible in that form.** If we need to accomplish something that does not fit into this pattern on a given Sunday morning, we have no hesitancy in abandoning the outline and substituting a more appropriate format. The worst trap we could fall into would be moving out of an inflexible traditionalism only to create a locked-in system of our own!

The Approach to God in Worship

As I stated before, the morning service is built around a purpose sentence which is carefully written by whoever is scheduled to preach. In a single statement this captures the thrust of the sermon. A characteristic, or attribute, of God is then chosen which corresponds with this emphasis. This selection is extremely important because the entire first part of the service will be centered around that specific attribute. For example, if the purpose sentence is "Building on the foundation of obedience to Christ's teachings will result in stability during life's storms," the attribute chosen would probably be that God is trustworthy. To emphasize God's jealousy fits the purpose sentence from the Jonah story: "With grand designs for this world, God assigns exceptional abilities to His stewards and jealously expects these favors to be used by them in accomplishing His purpose!" (A list of God's qualities for which we have extended Him our praise is given in Appendix A.)

As the ingredients for the first third of the Sunday morning service are planned, we ask ourselves, "In what way can we as a congregation best express to God our appreciation for this specific attribute? How do we attribute worth to (worship) God that He is by nature just, or holy, or everywhere present, etc?" If any unsuspecting member happens by the office during a staff meeting, he is often commandeered to share ideas with us. It is also not unusual for dinner guests to be asked, "If you wanted to praise God that He is love, how would you go about it?"

A. One of the normal ways in which we can praise God is **prayer.** We stipulate that if prayer is to be used during the time of worship, it must not drift into requests but must stay centered on crediting God for His exceptional qualities. Such praying should be very stimulating. We are in considerable agreement that most of the worship prayers (if they really are worship) intoned in the churches of our backgrounds are unplanned, uninteresting, and probably unheard by the people. (Quite possibly God isn't all that taken up with them either!) Somehow the sententious drone is a signal to tune out—to make a fast prediction on the score of the afternoon football game or mentally to serve the Sunday meal to waiting guests.

At Circle we want to make legitimate expressions of our deep appreciation to God for what He is. The invocation, therefore, far from being thrown together, represents insight and thoughtfulness. It is not unusual for a staff member without a preaching assignment to spend an hour or two in writing the invocation alone. In the examples given here you will note that these prayers don't include requests, they center totally on praising God for who He is.

> Father—
> The cry of our country from thinking people
> is not for law and order
> but for justice.
> Justice only reigns where mandates are fair,
> enforcement is adequate,
> and capable men sit in judgment.
> Admittedly, our laws fall short.
> More offenders escape detection than are arrested,
> and today, judicial halos come tainted.

We praise You, Father, that Your commands
favor no lobbying interest group.
As Christians we admire Your wisdom that
establishes guidelines for us that protect the
freedom of individuals without endangering society.
We are pleased to know that nothing escapes Your
attention and that someday, as reigning Sovereign
of the Universe, You will bring all to light.
We honor You further by stating that we believe
You to be an omnipotent God who is capable of enforcing
your judgments; and these will be fair because You
are omniscient.
You know not only the transgression but the background
of the transgressor.

You are infinitely just.
No greater justice can be imagined.
We worship You.
And unlike any other judge, You not only punish
the offender, You reward the righteous.
Thank You.
Amen

We try to make the prayers as meaningful as possible. During
the Christmas season while praising God as a congregation that He
is Love, I brought my three little children to the platform—Randall,
Melissa, and baby Joel. Holding the fat little number two son in my
arms, I began my prayer:

Father,
I come to You this morning a father like Yourself.
I appreciate Your gift of these children to me.
I love them very much.
If it were required of me to send any one of them
to a world I knew ahead of time would be hostile
and eventually demand their death,
I would not do it.
I consider myself to be a loving father.
You are a totally loving Father, and yet You
were not like I am.
You gave Your Son to a sinful world.
I praise You for Your love to me and to my family
and to all of us here that You did not act
as I would have.
But that in love you sent Christ into the world . . ."

One Sunday morning while Ka Tong was praising God for His wisdom and great understanding, a second person began to pray at the same time saying, "God, I am pleased that You can hear many voices at one time. Obviously, people in the congregation will have difficulty sorting out the thoughts the two of us are expressing, but I know You won't have such a problem. I praise You for Your wisdom . . ."

As the dual prayer continued, the truth of God's intelligence came vividly alive to the whole congregation, and I believe God responded well to what was being prayed, because we were demonstrating that we truly meant our praise.*

B. Music has traditionally been considered one of the foremost means of praise. As we have grown in our understanding of what God is like, we have come to believe there is a noticeable lack in hymnology regarding certain of God's attributes. Much has been written about His being all-powerful, wise, and holy, but what about the fact that God is personal or unique (the only one of a kind) or absolute? On occasion, having spent great periods of time trying to discover songs that are proper for certain attributes, we have finally had to resign the effort.

We are not above changing words, however. Often a hymn listed under Worship in hymnals does not really address itself to God but is more a testimony of what He has done. A typical readjustment might take place in the hymn

> God is love, His mercy brightens
> All the path in which we rove.
> Bliss He wakes and woe He lightens.
> God is wisdom. God is love.

In the change, the words become

> You are love. Your mercy brightens
> All the path in which we rove.
> Bliss You wake and woe You lighten.
> You are wisdom. You are love.

This may be considered nitpicking by some. But make the psychological differentiation between simply relating a friend's good

---

*More illustrations of worship prayers are given in Appendix B.

qualities to another person and actually telling that friend you appreciate his good qualities—"John has the most loving spirit," vs. "John, I appreciate so much your gentle spirit of love. It sustains me and buoys me, and there are days when I don't know if I could go on without your thoughtfulness." Then you will understand the subtle difference in worship that is so often lacking. Consequently, we force ourselves to address the words of praise to Him rather than allowing ourselves to be satisfied with chatting to one another about Him.

If we were to sing a song of testimony during The Approach to God in Worship I believe a dozen people would buttonhole me immediately after the service and want an explanation. I am glad for this. It shows they understand worship and appreciate it for what it is.

The more we have explored the adoration of God and familiarized ourselves with His qualities, the more we have discovered about Him. For instance, my background has always taught me that God is Creator. This is true, but it is only a partial extension of the total—that God's very essence is **creativity** and the creation is only one small outworking of His creativity. The source of man's true creative expression is rooted in the nature of God, and the Christian finds more and more creativity available to him as he aligns himself with the Godhead.

This particular discovery was amplified in worship one morning as the choir sang from the rear of the hall, "How Great Thou Art." The words to this hymn are overly familiar, but they were lent added depth and meaning when another sensory impression was added. One of our professional photographers had prepared a slide presentation which illustrated the words:

> O Lord, my God, when I in awesome wonder
> Consider all the worlds Thy hands have made.
> I see the stars, I hear the rolling thunder,
> Thy power through all the universe displayed.

Ken Semenchuk has his degree in cinematography from the University of Southern California, so anything he does in the visual realm is well done. The slides illustrated beautifully the measure and beauty of God's creativity—from the minute to the grandiose.

We are very pleased with the growth of the choir and their

increasing ability in a wide range of styles. Even so, there are rare occasions when certain songs cannot be performed by them due either to the shortness of practicing time or the lack of specific instrumentalists or even expertise. At such times we have found that the utilization of recordings can be most helpful. It is sad how many churches have closed their minds to the aid that technological tools can render. How foolish it seems to me that struggling congregations who cannot afford to invite professional Christian artists to their churches refuse to be open to benefiting by those same talents via recordings, especially when the records have been made for the purpose of ministry. To prefer third-rate talent or no music at all because of some ill-founded scruples seems a tragedy.

Worship music does not have to be heavy. Obviously, some of the finest written are classical in style, but there are Christian cultures that express worship in great spontaneity as well. One couple in the congregation expressed adoration to God for His sovereignty by singing "He's Got the Whole World in His Hands." Changing the words a bit in order to address them to God— "You've got the whole world in Your hands"—they began to clap the rhythm. (This spiritual like so many others seems to lose great feeling when adopted by staid white congregations.) After singing several verses, they invited the congregation to join with them on the remaining choruses. As a body, singing and clapping, we seemed to express most wholeheartedly our adoration for His supreme authority. Now clapping often occurs spontaneously when a song with much rhythm is used. Since we are not quite the "Shout Hallelujah, Brother," type, the handclapping seems to fit our style much better.

The congregation has often sung a praise hymn only to hear at the conclusion of a verse a trombone playing the same melody from the back of the auditorium. The singing stops between verses, the instrumental version continues, and the words just sung are flashed on the screen (by an overhead projector) to emphasize what we are speaking to God musically. It is unfortunate that instruments have so often been relegated to the evening service. It is like saying, "Well, you may have a musical gift, but it will have to be slotted into the Sunday night service because it doesn't fit the traditional morning pattern." But when praising God that He is rightful King or Sovereign, what could be a more natural sound than trumpets?

Perhaps it would be good at this point to examine the Old Testament Scripture for its attitude toward worship. When I compare the dull, formalized worship in most churches with the great gladsome expression of awe which characterized our fathers in the faith, I feel we have a long way to go to catch up with their example.

> Praise the Lord with the lyre,
>   make melody to him with the harp of ten strings!
> Sing to him a new song,
>   play skillfully on the strings, with loud shouts.
> (Psalm 33:2, 3)

And David and all the house of Israel were making merry before the Lord with all their might, with songs and lyres and harps and tambourines and castanets and cymbals.
(Psalm 81:1-3)

> Praise him with trumpet sound;
>   praise him with lute and harp!
> Praise him with timbrel and dance;
>   praise him with strings and pipe!
> Praise him with sounding cymbals;
>   praise him with loud clashing cymbals!
> Let everything that breathes praise the Lord!
> Praise the Lord!
> (Psalm 150:3-6)

> Clap your hands, all peoples!
> Shout to God with loud songs of joy!
> (Psalm 47:1)

C. Another means of expressing worship is through the use of **Scripture.** For this to be utilized properly as true praise, the Scripture should be addressed to God. Psalms are often fitting here. Responsive readings have been used traditionally, but because they never change in form they have become dull through repetition—preacher, then congregation, preacher, then congregation. Very simple adaptations can be made in this procedure. One side of the congregation can read, then the other. The Scripture can be scripted in the bulletin with the men reading powerful

portions, women the sweeter ones. The staff can read parts that
are more difficult and require practice. Some parts can be marked
unison; there can be soliloquys with hand-picked readers ready.
The possibilities are limitless. Churches haven't begun to do
enough with speech choirs, choral readings, dialogues, and mono-
logues. With all of these techniques related to Scripture, we can
lift our voices in meaningful and creative praise to God.

D. Giving can be an act of worship. This is true not only of the
offering, if it is included in this portion of the service, but also gifts
of any kind.

As preparation to praise God that He is life, we sent out a letter
in advance to the families of the congregation asking the children
to bring special gifts to the church for the service. The gifts were
to have had life or were to be alive. They were from the children
to God, an expression of appreciation for the fact that God is life
and the source of all life.

That morning in the time of worship, at a scheduled moment,
little children began to stream from all corners of the auditorium.
Some came steadfastly, greatly impressed with the solemnity of
their act. Others moved shyly. A few suppressed embarrassed
giggles. Each brought a gift of life . . . a shell, a bouquet of flowers,
a box of white mice, a pine cone, a fossil. Green plants were placed
on the table along with two parakeets in a cage. A box of salaman-
ders found its way beside a book. One boy brought himself and
drew up a chair to sit upon as a symbolic act of dedication. How
beautifully each gift prepared us for the message, "The initial sign
of renaissance in a society is the commitment of Christ's followers
to the **life style** He taught."

E. Variety and Change. In four years' time we have utilized
literally hundreds of new ideas that have helped us creatively and
meaningfully to express our adoration. Abandoned forms of corporate worship such as poetry are once again coming alive. The
poetry is even more satisfying when it has been written by someone in the church. The more we try, the more ideas there seem
to be to attempt.

We are working our way back to the time when worship was
begun by the loud agonized call of a ram's horn. How can we
praise God with the timbrel and the harp? How can we praise Him
on high-sounding cymbals? In what way can we properly use

dance? Where are the twentieth-century counterparts to our Hebrew forebears, those great men whose daily existence involved
concentrated acts of praise to God? We are discovering undreamed
of ways to employ the overwhelming talents of this single congregation to worship and to adore; and we are anticipating the discovery of more.

Each service continues to be different from the ones before it.
But it is imperative to stress that this is not an attempt to be different for the sake of being different. **We are not trying to be novel.**
We are trying to be meaningful, to discover exciting forms of worship. We are attempting to give expression to the abundance of
gifts that God has given to us. Paradoxically, the simplest services
are often the best, because they stand in quiet contrast to those
which are most complex. Their beauty and simplicity are deeply
touching.

The result of all this variation is that it has taught each of us to
be more open to method, to remain flexible in our attitudes of adoration, to find meaning in the unusual. One morning a comical illustration of this occurred. Every so often the Teamsters need to
schedule policy meetings on Sunday morning in "our" auditorium,
and they then make the basement area of their new office building
available to us. The change of meeting place is good for us, as we
have to adjust to the confusion and bustle. The children have to
find different Sunday school patterns, boxes of hymnals must be
transported the quarter block, and we have to change from piano
to accordion. It keeps us on our toes.

It was on one of these mornings when Ka Tong was praying,
that piped-in music began to play over the intercom system. It
continued for thirty seconds or so while Ka Tong (he fortunately
has his own built-in amplifying system) just waxed louder, until
at last someone found the right button and cut the interference.

That evening Milt and Sharon Feryance dropped past. "What did
you think of the background music in the service this morning?"
I laughed.

We all smiled as if this was just a part of the "let's change
locations this morning" game. Then Milt confessed, "You know,
I really thought it was planned. I figured sooner or later the reason
you did it would be understood, like so often happens!"

The more we shared his reaction, the more we discovered a

similar response from others. The unusual has become an extension of our worship, not a distraction.

God Speaking Through His Written Word

The second part of our morning service we have entitled "God Speaking Through His Written Word." While many ministers limit the impact of what they have to say to preaching, at Circle Church it is felt that the entire middle part of the service should emphasize the main thrust. Therefore, in preparation, we ask, "How during this time can we (1) best prepare the audience for the sermon, and (2) at its conclusion underscore what has been said through the use of a different tool?"

A. Preparation of Audience. While preaching on the fourth chapter of Daniel, I felt it was necessary for the people to attain a feeling of the grandeur of ancient Babylon in order to understand Nebuchadnezzar's pride and subsequent humbling by God. This story was being used to illustrate the main thrust, "Those who walk in arrogance, God is able to abase; but when we are humble in our attitude toward Him, God is pleased." After the worship and just prior to the sermon, a brief filmstrip on "Babylon's Glory" was presented which conveyed information pertinent to the topic and in a far more appealing way than I could ever have done verbally. I began the sermon not only with the enlightened understanding of the people, but with their interest as well. In preparation for that Sunday, the usual question was asked: "After the time of worship is there an additional way to prepare the audience for the sermon?"

If the biblical text is narrative, the various parts can be scripted for different voices, such as Luke's account of the wise men questioning Herod about the birth of a baby king. Contrast this type of communication to the normal pattern of beginning a sermon by reading the text.

Many times we have found secular sources to be especially effective. Scripted readings from the week's newspaper columns dramatically amplify the dilemma of man. Phrases of contemporary writers poignantly display the despair which is felt in today's world. While preaching on the millennial reign of Christ and that eventual Utopia He will establish, the topic of mankind's historic yearning for a perfect place was introduced by reading portions from a "Time" magazine editorial on Utopia which had appeared the preceding week. (Three members of the congregation who had read the preparation assignment in the bulletin called to tell me about the editorial.)

Since so much of our younger generation moves to the prevailing mood of music, even secular pieces can help to prepare an audience for the theme of the sermon. A few phrases from Burt Bacharach's "What the World Needs Now Is Love, Sweet Love," again by use of tape, is a perfect bridge to the purpose sentence: "My theme relates to the often-heard request of today's world. Much of popular music is emphatically stating that the world is starved for love. My emphasis today is: 'Christ repeatedly taught that His followers should demonstrate an attitude of love for others.' "

Of course we more regularly employ sacred music (congregational hymns, choir, solos, etc.) at this point. The general message of music used just before the message should be, "Having worshiped God, we are now anxious to hear Him speak to us. Let us open our understanding to His truth."

A simple prayer may fittingly introduce the sermon: "God, we have been praising You to the best of our ability, and we trust that You will accept what we have done as a sincere expression of our feelings, thoughts, and convictions. Now help us as we listen to You speak to us through our pastor as he opens Scripture. Give us insight into Your truth and a desire to apply it to our lives. Amen." Again, whatever is used during this time must result in a positive reply to the question, "Is this a means by which the congregation can be better prepared at this point to comprehend the message I am going to give?"

Preparing an audience for a lecture is about as basic to good programming as one can get, yet it is amazing how little this primary knowledge is applied. The countless situations where a congregation moves into a message cold are unbelievable. Recently, I was invited to speak in a very fine suburban church. My sermon dealt with the dynamic principle of Christians being a third force of reconciliation in our divided American society. I shared words of Christ that I felt related to war, poverty, and racial division. It was a vital and pertinent message! Before I spoke, however, a dear

lady sang about flowers and birds—pastoral allusions that even by
the wildest stretch of imagination had no bearing on what I was
saying. It is this kind of ludicrous contrast that careful planning
seeks to prevent.

B. Illustration of the Sermon. I feel very strongly that preaching
should not be limited to oration. With the immense number of aids
available today, a minister must take advantage of every possible
means to improve his listener's receptivity. Without exception the
main thrust appears in our bulletin on a special sheet which also
includes space for taking notes. If there are terms which need defining, these will be explained on the insert as well. Statistics
printed ahead of time eliminate the normal frantic search for a
pencil or the writing of lists in too short a time. Even the sermon
outline itself can be included.

Education statistics reveal that 10 percent of a subject will be
remembered if listening is used alone, 20 percent if seeing is used
alone, and 65 percent if seeing and listening are combined. It is
absurd, therefore, to overlook the teaching impact of visual aids.
Our overhead projector is constantly in use. It may display the
sermon outline, or it may project a biblical map on the screen for
geographic clarification. The slide projector can also amplify. If I
am talking about a contemporary well-known figure, his image can
be flashed on the screen. Multi-media presentations, light and
sound happenings—the possibilities are endless. So many techniques are being used and initiated effectively by the secular
market, and often to promote what is in essence anti-Christ. Why
can **we** not be wise communicators as well?

While working with the purpose sentence "Making proper requests of God demands forethought," I used a recording of Zero
Mostel singing Tevye's pitiful prayer in "Fiddler on the Roof." In
it he dialogs with God about the many poor people in the world
and states that though it's not a shame to be poor, it isn't a great
honor either. Tevye's plea is that he be a rich man, and he inquires
as to whether granting this request would upset some great eternal
plan. Explaining how characteristic such praying is even in Christian circles, I showed why it was not proper. How much more effective this was than simply stating that we often don't make proper
requests of God.

A good illustration of utilizing outside helps was exemplified by

a recent team-preaching sermon, "Building Blocks of Our Faith."
Attempting to be basic, we determined that an individual must
have four ingredients present in his "between Sundays" life: (1)
the study of Scripture, (2) private worship and prayer, (3) the influence of other Christians, and (4) involvement in ministry. In
discussion the staff decided that a team-preaching approach would
more satisfactorily amplify our thrust than a solo presentation. With
one person emphasizing each point, it would make the divisions
more distinct and the content clearer.

We hoped to further couple this with a visual approach for even
greater emphasis. Ka Tong thought of the Parker Brothers puzzle,
"Instant Insanity"—four building blocks with different colored
sides. The purpose of the game is to stack the blocks so that each
side of the column has all four colors showing. The idea clicked.
Large wooden blocks were made and painted by a man in the
congregation.

The central section of the service, "God Speaking Through His
Written Word," began with Ka Tong's explaining that for many
people, living the Christian life is a great puzzle, a spiritual struggle
somewhat like trying to accomplish the impossible. Then he
pointed to the four giant blocks, revealing the difficulty of stacking
them properly and why the puzzle was called "instant insanity."
He concluded: "What we are attempting to do this morning is to
give you the keys that unlock the secret of this puzzle and at the
same time give meaning to the puzzle of spiritual living as well."

One at a time, we shared a part of the topic, "The Study of Scripture," "Private Worship and Prayer," "The Influence of Other
Christians," and "Involvement in Ministry." As each man finished
he pasted the title of his emphasis on a side of one of the blocks
and put his block on the stack. When we had finished, the instant
insanity game had been solved as well as the puzzle of the "Between Sunday Spiritual Building Blocks." The truths had been
shared verbally and now they were visible on the front side of the
four blocks—a vivid illustration of the morning's message.

C. Underscoring the Sermon. The final consideration regarding
this middle portion of the service is "Can we emphatically restate
the point of the message in another way?" We are not asking,
"How do we get the people to respond to what has been said?"
That follows in the third section of the service. Rather, the question

is "Is there a method by which what has been preached can be underscored so the truth will become even more explicit to the congregation?" Most likely there will be some way to do this, but if it has to be forced or contrived, we prefer to reject it and proceed to the final part of the service.

One of our favorite methods is to employ Scripture. Since the major portion of my sermon preparation is limited to the study of Scripture, I usually have more than I can possibly handle in the twenty-five-minute preaching period. To reiterate the main thrust with the dynamic of additional Scripture is most powerful. Simply to place biblical passages on the overhead projector, allowing them to be read by each member silently, is also effective.

Christian literature, either current or classical, can be another tool to reemphasize the point of the sermon. We have often used excerpts from Joe Bayly's writings, selections from C. S. Lewis, portions of T. S. Eliot, or to travel farther back in time, sections from John Bunyan's "Pilgrim's Progress" and Milton's "Samson Agonistes" or "Paradise Lost." If extensive reading in certain volumes would be of further help, then we provide these books at the book table and recommend them from the pulpit. Poetry has been read, dramatized, and visually projected.

Another twist on the use of Christian literature was supplied by one of our members, Coleman Luck, Jr., whose experience in radio comes from having been the production advisor at a local station. Not content with simply reading from the story of George Mueller which was to amplify a message on faith, he put together a radio script. Utilizing members of the congregation, he taped the dramatic presentation with sound effects and played it following the sermon.

The time following the sermon is a favorite place for musical selections. As the lyrics restate what has been said, the special numbers suddenly have great significance. If the pieces are declaring truth, not responding to it (such songs are reserved for the third part), we often present several numbers in a row. The variations on this basic idea alone are endless. The choir can sing, smaller groups of voices can be used, music can be interspersed with readings of Scripture, and on and on. We are beginning to use the original music of our congregation. A single guitar accompanying a solo voice is inexpressibly lovely.

Secular material, both written and musical, can be of help in tying biblical truth to our present-day world. In a sermon which stated that the great need of the world is for love, the very commodity the Christian is supposed to have in abundance, we followed with an intriguing sequence. To demonstrate that the cry of the world is exactly for what had been preached, the song "Come on now, brothers," came on via tape recording. As it continued—"Let's get together, Let's love one another right now"—the volume was turned down and Ka Tong, at the back of the auditorium, began reading clippings from the previous day's newspaper.

> Barring last minute developments Sheriff Joseph Woods will resume evicting members of the contract buyers league early next week.

> Military sources said guerrillas firing rocket-propelled grenades and machine guns killed 7 South Vietnamese troops and wounded 23 others in an attack. . . . The defenders killed 15 of the attackers.

> Ralph Bellamy, 33, . . . was sentenced Friday to serve 100 to 199 years in prison for the murder of a Chicago patrolman . . . last December 27th. Criminal Court Judge Robert J. Collins ordered Bellamy to serve an additional 15 to 20 years for the attempted murder of another policeman.

> Meet the "Chicago Thirteen." They are not, as you might suspect, a collection of radicals in trouble with the law. Rather, they are an imposing array of some of the city's bigger private enterprises. They are also Chicago's biggest individual sources of air pollution.

At this point, a recording of "What the World Needs Now Is Love, Sweet Love" started to play with Ka Tong's voice intoning the names on the newspaper list in the background. "U.S. Steel Corp., Republic Steel Corp., Wisconsin Steel Division"—"It's the only thing that there's just too little of"—"Interlake Steel Corp.; Commonwealth Edison Company"—"What the world needs now is love, sweet love."

Then drowning out all these sounds the choir began to sing the prayer of St. Francis of Assisi:

Lord, make me an instrument of thy peace;
Where there is hatred let me sow love;
Where there is injury, pardon;

. . . .

O Divine Master, grant that I may not so much
Seek to be consoled as to console;
To be understood as to understand;
To be loved as to love . . .

We are fortunate to have so many students in the congregation with special abilities, and we attempt to utilize them in the services. One Wheaton College senior, Bonnie Barrows, had worked for months preparing her senior speech recital. She had carefully edited and memorized extensive passages from Catharine Marshall's bestseller, "Christy." Our examination revealed that much of it illustrated the main thrust of the series I was preaching on Christ's command to love others. Following one sermon in the series, she performed portions of it, in costume, taking about twenty minutes—another powerful method of reemphasizing the message.

When Ka Tong preached a difficult sermon, "As mature Christians make intelligent decisions about their future, they formulate God's will for their life," we anticipated problems in comprehension, and consequently programmed opportunity to ask questions. We specified that the inquiries were not to deal with response to the theme but to dwell on necessary clarifications. In order to keep more vocal individuals from monopolizing, cards were included in the bulletin for written questions. The staff collected these during a hymn, sorted them, and directed the most helpful ones to the platform at the appointed time. About fifteen minutes were given to this in the total service, greatly clarifying Ka Tong's thrust.

Many, many ideas can be utilized at this point in the service, but it must again be underscored that the purpose of any material which follows the sermon is to restate what has been said. If the idea detracts from the thrust of the message, eliminate it.

The Response of Obedience

The third portion of the morning service is the Response of Obedience. This, of course, is the time when we provide an opportunity for individuals in the congregation to respond in one way or another. As pastors we always ask ourselves, "What is it we want our listeners to do as a result of hearing our words?" If we are unable to answer that question, then most likely the sermon is not worth preaching.

One of the glaring deficiencies of many ministers is an inability to put sermons on a practical level. My wife and I recently took a weekend just to refresh ourselves, and had the rare opportunity to listen to someone besides Circle staff preach on Sunday morning. The content of the sermon was interesting because it was packed with numerous stories and illustrations. But when the man had concluded—his topic dealt with what a minister of God should be —by force of habit I immediately analyzed his words to see if they were practical for those who heard him. I couldn't think of any way to apply them nor could Karen!

Once again I was convinced of the need for disciplining oneself to determine exactly the kind of response desired. Rather than expound empty words of oratory that have no effectual relationship to a congregation, the pastor should make every effort to validate the message. The simplest way I know to do so is to ask, "What kind of response is it I want?"

Traditional methodology lumps all response under "invitation." But in many ways an "invitation" is the least helpful. When it is used and reused, aren't we implying that a person must walk to the front of the church to receive spiritual help? It seems to me that we then restrict the value of our sermons by limiting response to Sunday services, to the end of a sermon, to the accompaniment of an invitational hymn. Ideally shouldn't the application of the sermon be geared primarily to a daily, moment-by-moment reappraisal of one's present position before God? Apart from conversion, isn't this really the kind of response we are seeking—the mature development of the total being in his working, striving existence; not comforted by the security of the church womb but confronted by the tension of living? It is here that I need help most, in the day-by-day living of my Christianity, and it is at this point that I seek to make my message pertinent to my people.

At Circle we use invitations very infrequently. Still we find that great numbers in our congregation have grown by leaps and bounds, and there are continual conversions.

Almost always one of the ingredients in this third part is what we call "Suggestions for Life Response." This means that whoever preaches must prepare a separate time of approximately four to five minutes enumerating ways people can actualize what they have heard. We do not infer that these are the only ways in which application can be made, but our suggestions do encourage an attitude of mind which is conducive to response. Often this small list is harder to compile than formulating the sermon itself; but we believe in the necessity of this effort if the validity of the sermon is to be confirmed.

Suggestions for Life Response related to a sermon on conversion included the following: (1) to read the book "Peace with God" by Billy Graham—books were provided for those who did not have a copy; (2) to ask "What would I do if I wanted to become a Christian?" and after formulating an answer, to talk to the person who invited them to church to see what he did when he became a Christian; (3) to discuss the topic further in the Pastor's Class; (4) to make an appointment to talk to any member of the pastoral staff about the subject—their hours were given in the bulletin.

There are endless ways to provide suggestions for life response. I believe this one illustration gives enough of the flavor of what is intended that it will be unnecessary to develop the idea further.

Response can be provided by other methods. The most obvious way is to sing a hymn, a fitting expression for corporate response. Here again we are not satisfied to limit ourselves to the four or five overly familiar hymns which have been characteristic of the conclusion of services. We examine the words to discover one which truly expresses a positive commitment to what has been said that morning. Scheduled periods of silent meditation can initiate reevaluation and personal commitment. In contrast to this, we often open up the service to everyone saying, "We have now scheduled ten minutes during which we encourage any who would like to share briefly what God's Spirit has impressed on you to do so now." Then we wait as one by one from all sections of the congregation they stand to speak. This person has a portion of Scripture, another gives spontaneous testimony, and each of us, whether we have participated or not, gives inward assent to the outward expressions.

Once post cards were included in the bulletins which asked

people either to remind themselves "a dozen times, while observing society, that as Christians we inherit the role of significance in shaping it," or to talk "to another Christian about our inheriting the role of significance in shaping society." They were to check the appropriate box after completing the assignment, sign the card, and mail it into the church office. We received a large return—one came from South Africa, mailed by a member who had since left the States to film a missionary documentary—indicating again that this kind of suggestion helps to tie the truth of a Sunday morning experience to the everyday world wherever people are living.

If the offering is included in this final third of the service, it also can be a fitting way for people to respond directly to God. Rather than a dead time where clothes are adjusted and whispered chitchat is exchanged, it should be germane to the total. Words to the offertory can be printed in the bulletin. Slides which emphasize the morning's truth can be shot on the screen. Given the purpose sentence and the type of response desired early enough in the week, the pianist or organist can prepare arrangements which apply to the theme.

Our new black pastor, Clarence Hilliard, preached the truth: "As a Christian understands the relationship God maintains with him, he can better love himself and his neighbor." He was saying we are created uniquely in the image of God and are therefore people of great importance. The offertory that morning was a combination of "In the Image of God" with a sprinkling of the secular number, "I've Got to Be Me."

The Benediction is usually a time of saying to God how we are responding to what has been said. This can be done through prayers, by asking people in the audience to state verses of Scripture that relate to the theme, by a responsive reading, or with a solo voice singing a cappella from the back of the hall. The Benediction, like everything else, is planned. It does not just happen.

The Response of Obedience, then, seeks to provide meaningful ways of response for the overflow of hearts that have been touched by the Holy Spirit's presence on a given Sunday morning. It tries to allow immediate expression either on a private or corporate level, and also attempts to facilitate long-range, life-related commitment. It is patterned in various ways to meet the different levels of response which are present in any congregation.

The following illustration of the time of response was employed the Sunday morning my purpose sentence stated, "Christians need to understand that they are stewards of God." If you feel uncomfortable as you read, it may help to know that the staff was divided down the middle when I presented the following possibility in a Tuesday meeting. I suggested the use of applause as the response of obedience. Half were vehemently opposed to using it and the other half were adamantly certain of its validity. We employed the method with exciting results. Many relate to that morning as one of the most moving of their experience, and the staff members who had been against the idea have since reneged on their arguments.

The sermon developed the historic master-steward relationship in some detail. Then this New Testament analogy was applied to two basic areas of life—money and vocation. What follows is taken directly from my notes of that morning.

> Everyone serves some master, and the correct question to pose is, "What is your Master like?" That was always the great question in the mind of the literal slave. We are stewards, but the whole purpose sentence exclaims, "As Christians, we are **stewards of God!**"
>
> . . . This week I sought to discover a way to take this scriptural analogy of the master/steward and impose it upon our situation. . . . I want to blot out all the normal ideas people hold of God the Father and the person of Christ and reduce everything to this simple symbol of the master/steward as used in the Bible.
>
> ". . . If I were to introduce my congregation to the Master they serve," I thought, "if I were to remind them of all His true qualities, how is it I would want them to react? . . ." Did I want you to sing a hymn? No, that left me cold. Then I thought, "If we were all stewards and understood our Master, and He was actually here among us, and if God could be reduced to this simple master picture and could be properly introduced, what would we do?" I am convinced that we would all immediately stand and break out in spontaneous warm applause expressing gratitude to the One we serve.
>
> "That is what I want!" I thought. I will introduce our Master and although He will not make a physical appearance, I hope the introduction alone will make you enthusiastically say, "Yes, I am a steward! A steward of the most wonderful Master in the world!" . . .

In the Old Testament it speaks of the clapping of hands. Probably this is a rhythmic approach to God more in worship than applause. I don't want us to respond as though the Master were an entertainer of some sort, but rather as members of an "in-group" we are attributing worth to Him in gratitude for our relationship. In a moment I will ask you to stand and [applaud]. . . .

But now, fellow stewards, it is my privilege to introduce our Master, a man who is personally more interested in us as individuals than He is with His own projects. This is the One whose communication with His stewards is matchless. There is never a time we cannot immediately speak to Him and never a time when His work principles are not available to us. Those of you who know Him well realize that He has a loving sense of humor. Something I have come to appreciate about Him is that He isn't temperamental. His basic personality doesn't change from day to day. He is consistent. Our Master, unlike other masters, is good. In fact, His good is unsurpassed. He always does the appropriate thing and many times He goes beyond what we expect. Is that not correct?

He is trustworthy. If He gives His word, even to a slave, you can expect Him to keep it. I have never known Him to be sick or to look a day older or to take time off! Our Master is righteous and just in the way He operates, and yet He loves us all. So often He forgives us, and many times as our Master He goes that extra mile.

Then He is wise and His wisdom guides us. He helps us bypass many pitfalls we do not even see. We are stewards—more than that, we are slaves; but unlike the other masters, He doesn't call us in these ways. Do you remember what He calls us? He calls us sons and heirs! Maybe that is because He Himself has been a steward— because He humbled Himself taking on the form of a slave or servant. I guess this is partly why He loves and understands us so much.

He is the wealthiest of all the overlords, and He is the head of all the masters. He is the only one of a kind. Fellow stewards, let me present our unique Master, beyond description!

. . . let us stand and warmly express our appreciation to Him.

We stood, and we clapped, and with tears running down our faces awarded Him the response He so justly deserves.

It is necessary to reemphasize that The Service of Worship and Instruction is built around a central theme, the purpose sentence, which is a capsule form of the sermon. The entire program is then coordinated to fit that theme. The service contains three parts. First is The Approach to God in Worship, at which time we praise God for a specific attribute that relates to the purpose sentence. The second part, God Speaking Through His Written Word, is an unfolding by many means, including preaching, of the main thrust. Finally, The Response of Obedience serves to pin down that truth into the practical area of everyday living.*

Final Considerations

To avoid leaving the impression that we are inflexible in this form, let me repeat that we have great freedom to change the order of service, including the three parts. We refuse to be bound to a given pattern if something else will better facilitate our purpose. There are times when no one preaches. Music might be a better conveyor of the truth. Or there are times when Larry and the choir are given a rest, or where there is no music at all. There are even regular Sunday mornings when we encourage those who are interested to meet in small home services. When the church was small, intense intimacy was felt in shared experiences such as communion or corporate worship. But when growth occurred, it was easy for some people to lose the camaraderie of the sharing of worship when faced with so many unknown faces. Therefore, we try to provide enough occasions during the year for those who desire it to worship or observe communion on a more intimate level in their homes. Two Sunday evenings in advance are used for them to plan these times. Those who don't feel the need for such an experience come to the Union Hall and participate in the regular service.

Several final checks as to the morning service should be included before ending this topic. Appropriate material is chosen for use in the five minutes before the prelude begins. Because our 9:30 service is earlier than the established Protestant worship

---

*The complete service which is outlined at the beginning of this chapter is amplified in detail in Appendix C.

time, we have found it necessary to begin at 9:25 in order to remind our congregation to arrive earlier. A very special part of the service is put here—a musical selection, a dramatic or a visual presentation. This also helps to insure an attitude of quiet. (Facing the typical problem of parishioners choosing back seats, we tossed a cartoon visual on the screen, the caption of which read, "Happiness is coming to church early enough to find a choice back seat." It helped!) Whatever is used enables us to clear our minds in preparation for the worship which is to follow.

Another final check during the planning stages deals with the type of involvement the congregation has in the service itself. Singing hymns and giving offerings is not enough, in our minds, and we are continually trying to find additional ways to make people feel an integral part. It's easy to depend on the staff to participate because they are available, but a layman can do many jobs as well or better—preparing a historical introduction to the sermon, scripting and performing a multiple reading, giving a testimony of experience that amplifies the truth in the sermon. These are all on an individual level. Involvement on a corporate level is just as important—the holding of hands to express Christian unity, a responsive reading, the lighting of candles throughout the congregation to represent our position as lights in the world.

We are also constantly checking to see whether the children are adequately involved. We have used their rhythm band playing, "We Are One in the Spirit, We Are One in the Lord." We have asked teens to write and present a dramatic reading. We have interviewed them about their feelings toward God and have used them in duets. If in the process of the morning it is not possible to use children, then we try to make portions of the morning relate to them. Certainly it is as legitimate and probably more interesting to illustrate spiritual truth from the characters in "Sesame Street" as it is to use data from Spurgeon.

We check to see if we have involved all the physical senses possible. Again this pertains to the learning process, agreeing with the educational theory which states that the more of the five senses used, the more learning is increased. Hearing certainly is important, but hearing amplified by seeing insures greater learning and greater involvement. It is possible through feeling, such as holding hands, or through taste, such as communion, to involve people and increase their participation.

Once while discussing this matter the staff realized that we had never employed the sense of smell. We laughed about it and said it would be pretty tough to pull off. The outworking of that idea came the morning we praised God that He is Life. In the kitchens of the barroom of the Union Hall, fresh baked bread had been prepared prior to the service. At 9:30 following the prelude, the staff came to the platform and broke the loaves before the congregation. As the yeasty aroma lingered in the hall, these words were read:

> As the smell of bread is to a hungry man,
>   so is Christ to the searching soul.
> Today we are praising God
>   that He is the Bread of Life.

Later that same bread was tasted during communion.

The service is compiled without announcements. We do not intend for the continuity to be jarringly disrupted by, "On Tuesday afternoon the Boys' Clubs will be meeting. Please note that the place has been changed tonight to Adlar Hall, which is the second door on your right as you go down the front stairway. Incidentally, we are short some sponsors in this group. Please, fathers, do your duty toward our church boys and volunteer your services . . ." We also do not intend for a voice to intone, "Now if you will turn in your hymnals to page number seventy-three we will stand and sing . . ." These interrupt the flow of the meeting rather than aid it. Even a congregation with below-normal intelligence has the capacity to follow a bulletin. Isn't that the reason it was mimeographed to begin with?

Timing is important, since the Service of Interaction which follows needs an adequate period to accomplish its purpose. Each week as the service goes into its final form we put it together timewise to see how things are coming. A typical staff work sheet for a morning service might read as follows:

> Word Association (before service)
> Prelude (1 min.)

Call to Worship (1 min.)
Hymn (3 min.)
Invocation (1 min.)
Poetry (3 min.)
Choral Selection (3 min.)

Silent Meditation (1 min.)
Sermon (25 min.)
Musical Selection (3 min.)
Selected Readings (3 min.)
Musical Selection (3 min.)

Suggestions for Life Response (5 min.)
Hymn (3 min.)
Offering (3 min.)
Benediction (1 min.)
Choral Response (1 min.)

Total: 60 minutes

The normal response of people who hear all that goes into the preparation of this single hour on Sunday morning is, "My, but that's a tremendous amount of work." It's true, a lot of work is involved in each service, but I defend this for many reasons.

First, we are planning one such service a week instead of three. Second, the entire psychology of our congregation is one of excitement and anticipation toward church as a whole and toward the morning service in particular. Third, a great deal of our growth (and much of that growth is in the under-thirty age bracket) can be attributed to this positive psychology. Fourth, the learning which occurs is far and beyond my previous experience. (Can you tell me what was emphasized, preached, stated last Sunday? or in a month of Sundays?)

Fifth, the careful planning in the morning service has increased multifold the opportunities for members to utilize their gifts of the Holy Spirit. Since we are not content to do it the same way Sunday after Sunday, He is working in us a true expression of creative growth and power. Sixth, the congregation continually shares with the staff its growth in understanding of worship as a direct result of the service. Seventh, very little financial cost is involved (since for so long we had no finances to speak of and were forced to depend on human resourcefulness). I could probably go on and on, but these are the major reasons which give us validity for engendering so much energy for one hour a week.

Pastors may be thinking, "I don't have a team like you do. I can't possibly do the creative things that you are doing." But you do have a huge team behind you—your congregation, who up to this point have been limited in expressing their gifts. Pull them into the planning. For four years, the burden of this planning was on the shoulders of the Circle staff. During our fifth year, a portion of the congregation began to plan. Their enthusiasm and ingenuity, the quality of their talents and depth of their commitment, have been an inspiration to me. Ideally if a pastor can involve his congregation in the main functions of the church, it will be much better than having a staff who is totally responsible for those events.

"My people just wouldn't be open to many of these ideas, but they are expressing need for change." That is the unstated theme of this book. This chapter is full of methods which have been extremely pertinent and workable in our particular congregation. They will apply and be helpful to many groups; but to some they will be anathema.

The important thing is not to start with methods, but with a philosophy of how a church is supposed to function. From this philosophy you can build your methodology. In an established church don't change everything at once. Begin slowly. Choose a theme for the morning and coordinate your music so that it is appropriate. Maybe you can eliminate the announcements. But don't be afraid to change just because you can't change everything. A little at a time is most effective.

The chapter preceding this one tried to establish what it is a local church is supposed to accomplish. In the single meeting on Sunday morning we put into practice a part of that philosophy. Although prayer and interaction are present in that service, it is mostly corporate worship and the utilization of some of the gifts of the Holy Spirit that receive the major emphasis. Again, we do not feel that the methods (although they are extremely exciting to us) are as important as the philosophy. **How** you carry out your purposes is not as initially important as **whether** you **have** purposes you are trying to accomplish?

We are not insisting that everyone "do it our way." In fact one of the strange things about "the Church" is its similarity. Why are local congregations in South America so similar to the ones in North America? Certainly while we serve the same Christ and are part of the same body, the church is bound to have variations as differing as the cultures and climates in which it is found. More in-depth examinations than this have accused the missionary of trans-porting a cultural Christianity rather than a New Testament one. But is the missionary to blame? The Stateside church has very little variation in pattern either. It is time we allowed God's explosive, limitless, creative forms to invade His church.

Circle Church is different. We are plainly aware of that, and we hope that our experience will inspire and initiate similar situations —similar only in the fact that they are allowing God's Spirit to do His unique work in them. More than this desire, we are anxious and longing for the day when those very works begin to inspire and initiate creative new forms within Circle Church. Then we can to-gether experience the excitement of Psalm 122:1: "I was glad when they said unto me, Let us go into the house of the Lord" (KJV).

Chapter Five

*A time to talk, a time to pray,
a time to catch up.*

A Time to Talk

At Circle Church the traditional adult Sunday school classes do
not exist. Rather from 10:45 to 11:45 on Sunday morning we have
programmed a Service of Interaction which is designed to begin
fulfilling the inherent group need for sharing around the common
tie of the faith. A fifteen-minute break between the first and second
services allows time for people to greet one another and then re-
assemble for announcements and the introduction of visitors. A
great deal of spontaneity and hilarity is often evident during these
moments. I suppose much of it is immediate response to the beauty
and freshness we have experienced corporately during the time
of worship and instruction. Our spirits are high. We have been
challenged and uplifted, the results of which are often laughter and
warmth and a strong camaraderie.

After announcements are made, visitors are asked to stand.
While still small, we made a practice of having the first-timers give
their names and occupations, but our rapid growth soon frustrated
the benefit of this. Whereas before we could immediately meet and
become acquainted with the newcomers (and often bring them
home for a Sunday meal), it was now impossible to get our arms
around the twenty or thirty unknowns among us each week.

When the church began to receive publicity, we had many attend
who were simply curious. They were not interested in becoming
a part of our body, only in "seeing what was going on"—a phrase
I have trained myself not to resent. The solution seemed to be to
focus our attention, not on those who had come for the first time,

103

but on returnees. Therefore, while we still ask the first-timers to stand and fill out cards, it is the second-time visitors who are requested to introduce themselves as well as to share helpful background information. One of the staff members is assigned the responsibility of keeping track of these people, and if they return a third time he attempts to have them invited into the home of a member as soon as possible.

After these preliminaries, we go over the map of the auditorium included in the bulletin, which gives the position of the various discussion groups. Each discussion leader is introduced and invited to say a word about the topic and purpose of his group. Then we divide into as many as twenty to thirty small cells, one of which is the Pastor's Class.

The sole reason we hold our morning service at 9:30 is that the Pastor's Class can interact about the sermon. It would, of course, be impossible to discuss the service or the message before they were experienced. As a staff we invite any to attend who disagree with what has been said or done, who desire further clarification, or who simply wish to expand certain thoughts. Occasionally individuals come wanting to give testimony saying, "What was preached is so true, and I would like to share with others how it applies to my life."

The size of the Pastor's Class will vary from a few people up to a hundred. When the number is extremely large, the class is split into groups of fifteen to twenty, with other staff members or key people in the church conducting the discussion. Normal group size is between ten and fifteen, and the interaction always begins by asking each person to give his name plus a sentence or two of amplification—"I'm Anne Watson, I'm a nursing instructor and I'm leaving for South Africa in two weeks."

"I'm Don Dutter. I work with the Chicago school system as a psychologist."

"I'm John Visick, I'm single and interested."

These tags help us immensely in pinning facts to faces and often initiate immediate response: "Are you from Pella, Iowa? I'm from . . . ," and this mutual exchange is often continued after the discussion group.

There is a universal human tendency to forget a name the moment it is given, so I announce, "When we have completed the circle, I am going to call on one of you to name everyone." This simple gimmick usually insures avid attention when names and interest sentences are given, although remembering the sentences and forgetting the names is common. The process is important because it divides the unknown whole into individual personalities of the most initial sort and provides a jumping-off place for further relationships. We try to refer to one another by name: "Let's see now . . . your name was Bill, wasn't it? Well, I agree with what Bill said . . ." It never ceases to amaze me that at the end of the short session together, when someone is again put on the spot, almost invariably he can name everyone in the group.

The Pastor's Class is not structured like the other discussion groups where there is a given amount of material to be covered. In actuality, it is a sounding board for response to the previous hour. Sometimes I begin simply by asking why those people are in my class. We allow several comments to get on the floor

"Do you really think the Christian can have influence in this world? It's so big and the problems are so vast."

"I really dig what you were saying, but in my case I'm having difficulty applying the suggestions you gave."

"I had the most unusual experience this week which pertains exactly to the message this morning, and I just wanted to share it."

Then the group begins in the direction which seems most relevant to their common need.

We ministers have an ostentatious penchant for turning discussion groups into question-and-answer periods, so it is most important for us leaders to seal in our minds that the value of interaction is directly related to how many people participate, whether free interchange has occurred, and whether or not the group psychology has bent to the domination of one (the pastor). If something is asked directly of me—"What did you mean when you said . . . ?"— I will usually restate the question and then pose, "What does the group think I meant when I said . . . ?" By throwing it back to them I force involvement. This technique is also helpful if a derogatory attitude has been present on the part of a questioner. It takes me off the defensive, and the dynamic of the group usually handles the awkward moment with graciousness, firmness, and maybe a little humor. That pause gives me just enough time to formulate the exact words and loving manner in which I choose to answer.

Once discussion is allowed, one must be both open to and ready for the introduction of weird and offbeat ideas. I make it very plain that we are not interested simply in what people are thinking, but rather we are attempting to discover what the Bible has to say that pertains to our discussion. Once having shared this at the beginning of the Pastor's Class, a university student stated that although he enjoyed the church immensely he wasn't hot on going to Scripture as the final authority.

"Do you have another suggestion?" I asked. Yes, he thought his own intellect would be just as suitable. Turning to the rest of the group, I asked them if they wanted to discuss the morning's topic with Ralph's intellect as the base for final determination. No one wanted to.

"Would you have another suggestion, Ralph? The group doesn't think the first was a good idea." He said he was willing to discuss with Scripture as a base.

This is the only time when I have led the class that anyone objected to using Scripture as authority. In fact, the younger mind set seems to be one of eagerness to discover what the Bible has to say. Parenthetically, it is amazing to me that in the years of Circle Church, with this open invitation to explore verbally, with all the university and student types who attend, many of them non-Christian, there have rarely been questions asked relating to apologetics. The most fascinating topics seem to be foundational matters which relate to a basis for faith. It is far more likely they will ask, "Well, how does one become a part of the kingdom of Christ?" than, "How can you prove that the Scriptures were written at the time you assume?"

If I could choose one method which would guarantee a drastic change in the pastorate, which would initiate vital, practical sermonizing, which would close the clergy/laity gap significantly, it would be to conduct a Pastor's Class week after week. Invite open, honest discussion. Welcome disagreement. Such a class has shaken my whole approach to the ministry, for no one benefits from this procedure as much as the paid staff.

We approach sermon preparation with fear and trembling. There is no place for a last-minute "putting together of a few thoughts." The group must be faced afterward! There are no unconsidered ideas thrown randomly into the pot. The group will be waiting!

There is no capricious searching for nice illustrations to pad a sermon. The group certainly will demand, "That illustration didn't fit your sermon. Why on earth did you use it?" Many has been the time I have longed for bed and pillow around 1:00 or 2:00 on Sunday morning, but I have stayed up the necessary hours—sometimes throughout the entire night—just because I was fearful to face unprepared the people waiting in the Pastor's Class. Yet the agony is well worth it, since there is nothing so immensely satisfying as feeling that your personal pulpit ministry is deepening in maturity.

The immediate feedback is invaluable. This is something of which few ministers are able to avail themselves (except for those fortunate enough to have an honest and vocal wife; but even her criticism is not as broadly based as the composite efforts of a diverse group). With the Pastor's Class following the sermon you are instantly aware of what the people have heard.

Sometimes when the discussion is slow to start I will ask, "Would you share with me what you thought I was trying to emphasize in the sermon this morning?" This is an extremely healthy process. If there has been misunderstanding, it can be clarified and is not left to fester. It allows time to build great understanding on the part of the congregation toward their staff and on the part of the staff toward the congregation. Often I am able to prepare future messages based on the needs and desires which have been expressed.

Pragmatically, this concept has also eliminated the necessity for a tremendous number of calls. The normal route of the newcomer is to attend the Pastor's Class. This way the staff gleans information which slips out in the course of discussion. As visitors return, they are amazed to be called by name, surprised by the personal touch displayed. If they continue to attend and show interest, the pastoral staff usually entertain them as soon as possible in **our** homes. These initial encounters seem more natural to me than forced home visitation.

The very fact that a minister will submit himself to examination increases the confidence of a congregation in him. He is not trying to hide behind his position, is not afraid to admit to error or to work from weakness. An audience listens more closely knowing that dialogue is open to them. There is great value for them to hear their pastor say, "You know, you have a good point there and I appreciate your sharing it. If I preach on that topic in the future I would like to adjust it to the suggestions you have made."

While the Pastor's Class is in session, a continual low rumble caused by hundreds of voices reminds us that other groups are in process too. A statement in the bulletin reads, "Views expressed in the interaction groups do not necessarily reflect those of the church." Perhaps this indicates the make-up of the groups. The people are from every background imaginable, and not everyone talking is going to be a Christian.

Topics for discussion are chosen a minimum of two months in advance, although with little difficulty we can add last-minute subjects as we feel need for them. The range on a given Sunday morning can be vast, making it difficult for an individual to choose in which group he would like to share. (I personally feel this is a good problem to have to face. Scratching one's head and bemoaning the fact that "they all sound so interesting, I wish I could go to every one," is a great improvement over the semireluctant attitude usually displayed toward the average adult Sunday school situation.) On some Sundays the groups may all be based on the same general theme, if not the identical topic.

When the classes have been explained and locations have been assigned, people pick up their chairs and begin to form into small circles all over the auditorium. There may be as many as twenty to twenty-five groups, and the sound of a myriad voices speaking at once settles over the hall. Chairs are drawn closer together, voices modulated to the correct level, and soon each individual is absorbed. Every now and then laughter bursts from one of the groups, unaware of the refreshing interlude they have bequeathed to the room. Laughter is a beautiful thing to hear from God's people and we have more than our share.

The objective of the interaction groups is not exclusively academic. Possibly as great a purpose is to get to know one another as we converse around our common spiritual interest. This is one reason why so much stress is placed on the introductions. Our regulars try to keep this purpose in mind, try to reach out, to touch, to know those people in the group. In small groups relationships can be quite intense. At the end of the hour, even though the topic has not been exhausted, the people should know more of one another. Doubts have been shared, a view of unique striving has been caught. Someone has achieved, and we have hurrahed them. Another has determined to lend a hand.

One Sunday morning I was approached by a Christian Education professor after the time of discussion. "That was an interesting group, but we certainly didn't get very far into the topic."

I asked him how much he felt he had learned about the people who were in the circle during the discussion.

"Quite a bit," he replied.

Then a major purpose of the group had been accomplished, I pointed out to him.

It is hard to slip out of the traditional Sunday school frame of mind which is basically content-oriented. Many complaints have been registered that forty-five minutes is just not enough time— and it probably isn't for discussion related solely to learning. Yet, when I am in groups with sensitive Christians who are listening for needs as the people express their thoughts, I see fantastic human interchange accomplished. There is enough time for that!

This is not to say that we devalue learning as a goal. We couldn't possibly, with the type of curious, event-conscious, idea-aware group that makes up Circle Church, and we are continually evaluating this area of our life. We are discovering strangely enough, however, that groups which draw a conclusion often don't accomplish as much as those which remain open-ended.

One lady, new to our ways (not an unusual state), attended a class on "What Is the Mature Christian Woman Like?" At the end of the discussion she was quite upset that the group had never come to a conclusion. On Monday morning she phoned expressing her discomfort. "What they should have said was . . ." and she gave some conclusions.

On Thursday another call came from the same woman. "I have been thinking about this for quite awhile now, and I believe that this is what a mature Christian woman should be like. Could you pass it on to those who were responsible for the class?" She began to read several passages of Scripture for me. If the class had shared those same thoughts on Sunday, I asked her, would she be as excited about them as she was now? "Probably not," she admitted.

That is one reason we are not grief-stricken if a topic is not totally covered in the interaction groups. The open-ended format encourages further thinking—even if it is done out of aggravation! The ideas become personal, not just the assimilation of a leader's study. They are original, initiated by the thought struggle of the individual.

There are always a few people who either are reluctant or find it hard to contribute in a group setting. Yet we want them to feel as much a part and to benefit equally with the more loquacious types. Nearing the end of discussion, I usually say, "Now Jane and Darrell and Alex have not said anything, and we want to make sure that everyone has a chance to comment. Would any of you care to share with us?" Often the quietest individuals have the most interesting remarks to make. They have been thinking as rapidly as the rest, and have just needed a little encouragement. Those who have nothing to say, say so.

Circle Church has more than its share of creative individualistic types who give the impression of self-assurance and confidence. It can be a threatening experience for the person who is excruciatingly shy, not yet certain of who he is or where he wants to go, to be thrown casually into the stimulating mental exercise of many discussion groups. Yet, it is these very kinds of persons, the unsure, the uncertain, who most desperately need the ministrations of the group. One young girl recently came into the office and shared some thoughts which thrilled me.

"I've sat in discussion group after discussion group," she told me, "and never had anything to say. I was interested and learning. When the leader would ask if I had anything I wanted to say, I would just reply, 'No.' I don't think I've ever thought on my own! I just accepted everything that was told me. But you know, I really would like to contribute in those groups—to learn to think by myself."

Since then she has taken Bruce Larson's "Living on the Growing Edge" and "Dare to Live Now" and read them carefully. She is a very shy and quiet girl, but several Sundays back I was amazed when she responded during a morning service to the question, "What do you feel is the basic need of the church?" Standing to her feet before the whole congregation she stated, "To be more interested in other people and to help them develop their gifts!" The act was symbolic of her own struggle for growth.

Ruth is not an isolated example. Such growth and change happen many, many times.

On a purely mechanical level, we vary the sharing group topics
from month to month. They may have a strictly biblical approach,
such as a discussion of various aspects of Christ's Sermon on the
Mount: "What is the Christian's attitude to be toward worry, toward
material possessions, toward judging, etc?" Or they may be topical,
discussing how the Christian faith relates to such current issues as
abortion, pacifism, sex education in the public schools, violence.
With growth, we have had to limit the discussion groups to four
major elective areas running simultaneously for a period of three
weeks. An individual is, therefore, able to choose three out of the
four. These major groups are then subdivided into many small
groups that will each accommodate from eight to twelve people.

Each pastor is assigned one monthly discussion topic and it is
his job to see that an adequate number of leaders are prepared. He
meets with these people either in the office or in a home, and they
spend an evening in discussion   a sort of dry run—to see how the
topic can be handled adequately. Then the leaders make further
personal preparation in order to be able to conduct the group. The
basic key to the effectiveness of the circles is the ability of the
leaders. To assist them, we keep a file of magazine articles from
both secular and religious publications, which serves as a basic
reference guide for research.

It is important that the leader be trained to ask the right type of
questions. For instance, while discovering truths from James 1, the
leader can ask, "What does James mean in chapter one, verses
two through four?" If he does, he will receive academic answers.
Or he can ask, "Are any of you presently facing a trial (as James
writes about in chapter one, verses two through four), and could
you share this with us? Then we'll see if we can figure out how
these verses apply." Then a good basis for the type of discussion
we are seeking has been established, and the group can begin to
move forward.

As with the rest of the church program, variation is the key theme
in the interaction groups. While preaching from the book of Daniel,
the people discussed each chapter one week **before** I expounded
on it. Another member of the staff had them discuss a chapter
of James **the same day** he preached from it. Current books on the
Christian market, or secular books that in some way relate to our
faith can be the basis for good discussion, with a prerequisite

established, however, that the material must be read before anyone
is allowed to attend. Favorites among our congregation are works
such as those by Francis Schaeffer. Perhaps, if we anticipate that
the sermon material will be difficult or controversial, we will schedule discussion for nothing but reaction to the message—in other
words, having twenty-five Pastor's Classes.

We've held discussions on the topic "The Needs of Our Neighborhood," and arranged for groups to walk through the black
ghetto, to drive around the medical center, to visit Circle Campus,
to go into Skid Row, to view the area where neighborhood work is
going on. After thirty minutes we reassembled to discuss briefly
how we could most effectively meet the needs of these communities.

Along with the interaction groups that are held in the main hall,
we usually conduct a lecture class in the balcony. It helps to re-
lieve the congestion downstairs, and there are certain topics that
lend themselves to guided expertise rather than to open discussion.
Having scheduled a Christian clinical psychologist to direct a
three-week lecture series on marital problems, we then invited
those who expressed more complex needs than could be handled
in the Sunday morning sessions to register for extended evening
counseling in someone's home. Certain individuals in the congregation have specialty areas—such as our present Council chairman, John Hiltscher, whose background is urban architecture—and
they are able in a unique way to relate their interest to the church.
Usually the lecture will last for about twenty-five minutes with a
period for questions following.

The Service of Interaction is intermittently spaced with approximately one special Sunday a month. We might invite a guest
artist to have a musical concert, or even better, recitals are often
given by our own members. Joint recitals with two or three individuals performing are much appreciated, and we are in the process of planning our first children's musical. Panel discussions are
another possible "special," as was the case when we had whites
and blacks discuss the merits and demerits of the "Black Manifesto." Debates on topics can be helpful. We can have a film showing for the entire congregation, or one that is on an elective basis.

One of the most appreciated second hours has been when we
simply provide opportunity for unstructured fellowship. Coffee and
sweets are brought by the women, and we use the time to talk with

all those who seem to get away from us Sunday after Sunday.

A final change of pace comes at the end of each quarter when the normal groups are set aside, and applicants for membership are interviewed as to their spiritual background and asked why they want to become a part of the congregation.

What have we learned from participating in four to five years of interacting around the common topic which binds us together, our faith? The general principles seem to be:

1. **It is almost impossible for sensitive Christians not to respond to articulated need.**

I am sometimes overwhelmed by the immediate "burden-bearing" which takes place not only in the groups, but continues into the nitty-gritty of the week which follows. Much of it we are not conscious of until many months later. This is one of the most exciting dynamics of the Christian community in which churches are not participating, simply because there is no direct way for its members to express personal and intimate needs in a nonjudgmental atmosphere. I am not implying that people will blurt out intimate problems just because they are sitting in a circle. But is it natural for a person to pick a class on worry instead of forgiving or judging if he doesn't have some need in this area? If the leader is personal and honest, the chances are strong the others in the group will be as well.

This very principle in action eliminates much of the counseling which occurs in the pastor's study and transfers it to the lay level. There is a certain amount of therapy within the group itself which may occur, particularly when sensitive Christians are present. I love to see this dynamic in action—the disquietude which settles on a group when sudden tears are present; the hand which reaches to comfort another; the loving humor which counterpoints too intense expression; the involved twosome who have remained after dismissal to untangle disagreement. This is church vitality at its finest.

2. **Differences, whether of personality or on the idea level, should be a means of binding us closer together in love rather than severing us in conflict.**

The mark of the Christian group is the manner by which the

group holds each other in esteem. "By this all men will know that you are my disciples, if you have love for one another" (John 13:35). We have been told to pattern our love after Christ's, and yet He has a great advantage over finite humanity in that His understanding of individual lives is complete. Our partial knowledge of our brother is often the source of our difficulty in loving him.

This then has been the major prerogative for discussion: to understand, to accept, to know, to love. Despite personality differences, conservative or liberal leanings, economic and cultural persuasions, the tentative and often awkward groping for enlightenment has continued. Its most basic, broad-based form is in the discussion groups.

Too long the church has avoided controversy, equating it with disunity. There is bound to be disagreement within our Christian framework, but that does not mean we can't continue to feel spiritual love for each other. How often we say, "I really disagree with that approach," or "I don't think your ideas are right because they aren't scripturally valid." The deepest kind of love is able to embrace the diversity of opinions, to appreciate each person's right to think for himself in the way he chooses, to affirm the struggle for learning and Christian growth of which these processes are so often an indication. We have to try to keep controversy out of the personal level and use it to achieve; but there is no reason why it can't be a healthy exchange!

Perhaps a good example of what occurs so often ensued during our panel on the "Black Manifesto." Very strong disagreement arose between a key white member of the congregation and Mel Warren who is black. The point at issue seemed to originate from their differing racial acclimations. The two sides were adamantly expressed and strongly felt, yet the disputation ended with the loudest members on both sides embracing and saying, "I disagree with you violently, but I want the people here listening to know that I love you deeply."

When we understand one another, we find that we can love one another—despite disagreements which may arise in outlook. In fact, we are bound closer to one another because of the process we have gone through to achieve that love.

Like any other social situation, we have our share of misfit personalities, people whose self-fixations render them obnoxious to others. Yet we seem to be achieving a higher and higher level of tolerance which, after its initial sway, gives way to an awareness of responsibility. "Can you tell me what you know about so-and-so? I'm having a terrible time understanding him." "How do you think I could help her?" "Maybe we should invite them for dinner."

Because of a fear of disunity, congregations have too long avoided controversial topics like the plague. Yet the real world is awhirl in controversy, and if we deny our members the right to hammer out their beliefs in the receptive and helpful atmosphere of the church, aren't we doing them a disservice when they move out from its shelter to confront who knows what?

3. Using Scripture as authority keeps the groups in check.

One reason we are not afraid of divergent opinions presented in the discussion groups, is that we use Scripture as our authority. Nor are we afraid of controversy. Within the Christian body with its belief in absolutes, stability will sooner or later be represented —no matter how far out some proposed ideas may have been. Every so often we'll find ourselves following a tangent only to be arrested by someone's asking, "Now just a minute, what is the scriptural position on this?" Whammy! Everything comes suddenly back into focus.

Many churches within the Chicago area have been caught up in the charismatic movement with unfortunate results for some. I was present when a newcomer warned against any discussion on speaking in tongues as he felt it was "too hot a topic." He was immediately corrected by someone who said, "That's what we need to talk about then. We're not in trouble if we talk about a controversial topic; we're in trouble if we can't talk about it. Let's find out what the Bible has to say!" I felt the same way. After several years of experience, I think that, as a pastor, I can trust any topic to the leveling influence of a Christian group which assents to Scripture as authority.

4. The discussion groups serve as an initial phase for deeper Christian encounters.

When we were small (from twenty-eight to two hundred) we experienced intense relationships within these symposiums. Within the period of a few months, we gathered a goodly knowledge of one another because we would meet and remeet in the framework of discussion. This, combined with the large percentage of attendance at the prayer cells and an inordinate amount of entertaining, all helped us to experience a sense of community which was excitingly new.

Then came growth. We were overwhelmed by new faces in what had been our loving and intimate society. It was nothing to attend elective after elective and rarely encounter a well-known relationship. With growth, not nearly as large a percentage attended the prayer cells, and hospitality continued on a level which was most frustrating, trying to keep up with all the new ones.

Suddenly, we who had been thrilled by our Christian fellowship began to hear cries of "Superficiality!" Many old timers began to leave after the morning service. A dichotomy developed! Newcomers, who felt as though a dam had been broken releasing them to meaningful sharing around topics related to faith, sided with the more gregarious members who loved a "gang" (the more the merrier), who enjoyed meeting people, and who felt comfortable in group situations. Both were immensely satisfied with our second service. Others, however, longed for deeper relationships which they equated with more time spent together, a stable group, and an extended ministry of sharing.

It was a natural thing for interaction to be most affected by sudden growth, and we have had to make adjustments in thinking at this point. The discussion groups are the initial phase in our encounter. They are extremely effective when viewed on that level and, as has been stated, a great deal of ministry occurs within or stems from them. More supportive relationships can be developed in the prayer cells, during extended times of hospitality, or as we participate in church projects. The discussion groups are where we meet, where we become acquainted, where we garner a few clues as to personality.

After people have participated in interaction groups for several years they begin to feel much more secure about their faith. Christians can pretty well handle most problems with a minimum of discomfort once they know well their base of operation. Then unless these same individuals keep in mind the equally important purpose of the groups—to get to know one another—it is easy to feel that the discussions are not as valuable as they once were. Talk becomes cheap. Consequently, the mind set of such members is most important. We are continually receiving precious lives from God's hand—people who are searching, seeking, and finding great meaning at Circle. Many of them desperately need personal ministry. Many are struggling with the basics of faith. (As one member stated, "I'm at a more mature point in my rebellion than many of them are!") It is to these that we who have gone further down the road must extend our experience, our love, our relationship.

Pastors who have been in groups where I have spoken invariably ask, "How can we begin doing this? We have pews. We can't change our Sunday school system overnight." I try to stress that they not attempt to emulate what we are doing but adapt our principles to their situation. First of all, they have to make that mental adjustment which insists that meaningful interaction is an important function of the church. Then possibly they can provide some elective classes on an adult Sunday school level which center around discussion. Maybe they can schedule opportunity for the congregation to discuss the sermon with the preacher, and then program further change, in proportion to the response of the congregation.

For us, as we began to interact effectively over a period of time, our name, Circle Church, took on a second and more satisfying meaning. We had chosen it originally because of our geographic location, but now it came to symbolize something deeper, something which expressed the essence of our whole. A poem which we have used often in the worship service expresses this in part.

> He drew a circle that shut me out—
> Heretic, rebel, a thing to flout.
> But love and I had the wit to win:
> We drew a circle that took him in!
> (Edwin Markham, "Outwitted"*)

A Time to Catch Up

Perhaps one of the basic faults of the traditional church has been its ingrownness due in large part to the overwhelming number of meetings a "spiritual" member is supposed to support. One of

*Used by permission of Virgil Markham.

the major complaints of that small group which originally met in analysis of "The Church" was this very "meeting-fixation." We didn't see how a Christian could spend practically every evening within the physical confines of the church building and still be able to develop a nourishing family life, establish relationships with friends outside the pale, or even have adequate opportunity to grow in a personal knowledge of God.

This is essentially what our Sunday night planning now seeks to allay—the purloining of unnecessary evenings from the bountiful living of our congregation. The attitude isn't "Let's be careful not to bother the Christians with too many demands to live for Christ," but rather "Let's cut the Christians loose to be the church in the world."

When Circle Church started, our philosophy was that the Sunday morning service would center on the vertical man-God relationship, while Sunday evening would deal with the horizontal of man's relationship to man. We rapidly discovered, however, that the two are impossible to segregate. Christ told us " 'Love the Lord your God with all your heart, soul, mind, and strength.' This is the great first commandment. The second in importance is similar. 'Love your neighbor as much as you love yourself' " (Matt. 22:40, Taylor). So often the way we relate to God is distinguished by the way we relate to mankind, and the reverse is also true.

After we dropped this uncomfortable dichotomy, the Sunday evening meeting floundered for a while without purpose. For those of us who insisted on definition (mainly David Mains), who had pigeonholed and demarcated, circumscribed and prescribed, it was a little embarrassing to have this hour just floating vaguely around. Finally we became resigned to having one meeting which was basically a catch-all (capitalization might help: Catch-All). It became rather like the homemaker's proverbial closet—a place of utmost practicality that company is not supposed to open.

Usually we begin around 6:30, but the time is not binding. We may be in the Union Hall if the anticipated group is large, or the church office is often used to accommodate a smaller number. It is more likely, however, that homes (one or several) will be used, as they are definitely preferred by the congregation (and by our Union janitor). If many houses are involved, a common topic can tie together the different locations, or each may do their own thing.

The purpose on Sunday night is to service the needs of our supportive membership. This may be the most important way it is "a service." If it best facilitates our needs not to schedule a meeting, we leave the evening open. If the choir needs extra time to prepare for concert work, Sunday evening is the occasion.

This outlook has assisted us greatly in fulfilling our desire of releasing the church to interact within the world. For example, when we began we realized that not only did many of us have difficulty communicating our faith, but few of us had cultivated in-depth friendships with people outside our church-oriented community. Several Sunday evenings were spent sharing ways in which we could profitably express our beliefs, culminating in another Sunday evening when the church met, not in the building, but in their individual homes. Each member had prayerfully invited **for dinner** some acquaintance to whom he wished to extend companionship. During the week we all remembered one another in prayer, as well as the next-door neighbors who were considering divorce, the classmate who had attempted suicide, the international student who was lost and bewildered by his Stateside visit, and others.

The next Sunday night we met again to report on progress and found great commonality of experience. One of the most frequently noted was the simple matter of deciding whether or not to say a prayer before the meal! The emphasis proved very helpful. If the same approach had been scheduled for a series of week nights, however, it probably would not have gotten off the ground.

This attempt confirmed our general consensus that evangelism is best done on a one-to-one basis within the framework of proven interest and friendship. This need not prevent us from meeting together in a corporate attempt at sharing our faith. One Sunday night in particular we invited friends to the Union Hall for a specal concert which had been prepared by the choir. The entire ballroom had been set up like a coffee house with chairs grouped around many large round tables. Dessert was served at the appointed moment and we found that much of the conversation which occurred centered around the church, and more specifically, man's encounter with God.

It was always an enigma to me that in the churches of my background Sunday evening was considered "The Evangelistic Service," when week after week no outsiders were present. Without blinking an eyelash, the leader would extend the invitational hymn time and again, with rare response ("After all, we never know when God is working in the heart of a man"). Why haven't people admitted that this practice is usually ineffectual? Why haven't congregations demanded to be released to do grass roots evangelism in their homes at least occasionally on Sunday evenings?

Some friends of ours, he is a hospital administrator with a young and lively family, live in an exclusively new section of a nearby Chicago suburb. Balking at the incongruity of the traditional Sunday evening identity, they established a neighborhood Bible study. This pragmatic approach met with great success—they were suddenly participating in a true witness effort. But you can be sure that many in their church looked askance at their plan—not that they were holding a Bible study, but that they were doing it on a Sunday evening!

Through many of these episodes, our definition of evangelism has been broadened to include more than just the act of counseling which ultimately assists a person in conversion. We consider the effort of evangelization to include all the milieu which surrounds this occurrence—the feeding of hunger, the reaching out to emotional wounds, the establishment of relationships, the assurance of sincere interest, the sustained follow-up. Hospitality is one of the most pertinent and at the same time most overlooked tools of outreach. We consider the person with the developed gift of hospitality to be on a par with the individual who is able to exercise a gift of leading people to Christ. Often the two go hand-in-hand. I personally am an example of the latter, but I would not be able to exercise this gift effectively had needy individuals never been entertained in the homes of other Christians, invited to church, and included in activities. This is an example of the interdependence of the body which our Sunday evening services seek to assist.

Hospitality needs to be extended as well on the level of the Christian community. Circle Church has practiced this kind of ministry far above the average church. I suppose much of this is related to the need expressed by the younger generation for "real" interpersonal commitments and by their deemphasis of the material in light of the human. We have had some quasi-commune attempts and would like to see this continue on broader levels. But mostly we have seen the life of our community extended and deepened by sharing meals together within our homes. Simply, this relates to Sunday evening in the fact that we often schedule Hospitality Nights for this precise purpose.

A few outstanding examples of hospitality in our previous traditional church experiences were so effectual in ministry toward Karen and myself that they literally transformed our attitude as to the value of this area of ministry. Yet prior to the establishment of Circle, to be entertained even as a staff member was the exception, and members had little time open for one another.

A Sunday school class in the Wheaton church employed an excellent solution to this dilemma. They systematically mixed their members so that groups met in different homes for dessert and coffee after the evening service. It was effective, and yet it could have been even more so if the validity of the need to share community in hospitality had been recognized on a total church level. This would have resulted in a consistent cancellation of the evening service, a mixing of **all** age levels, and the utilization of an extended period of time—the entire evening—rather than the weary moments which usually are experienced at the conclusion of "the day of rest."

Off of the soap box and on with some particular illustrations of our philosophy toward the Catch-All. When the discussion groups are dealing with society-related problems, we often hear the need expressed for intense Bible study. The reverse is also invariably true: when we stress in-depth Bible study, requests for topically related subjects begin to come. The evening service can counterbalance the morning emphasis. At a time when examination of Scripture was in order, several nights were spent discussing some parables of Christ. Members were assigned to various locations and we asked each hostess to prepare food which would amplify or illustrate the passage. When we discussed the parable in Luke 13 about the fig tree planted in the vineyard, each hostess served figs and other fruit. "What father among you if his son asks for . . . an egg, will give him a scorpion?" (from Luke 11) resulted in the preparation of eggs of one kind or another, the consensus being they were easier to fix than scorpions! Sharing together we related individual needs in an unhurried manner to what had been read.

The open Sunday evenings are a most refreshing interlude, such as holiday weekends when students are away and family plans are in order. Especially appreciated are these times with the children and simply to relax. On occasion, instead of having a service of our own, we will encourage our people to attend another church. This gives them a healthy perspective as to the value of other congregations, and also of our own. Recently members signed up with Pastor Hilliard to go to a black church and participate in that service. During an extended citywide crusade such as one conducted by Billy Graham or Tom Skinner, we cancel all our evening services and encourage attendance at their afternoon rallies.

Feeling keenly the presence of many internationals in our midst, we thought it would be helpful if we had a better understanding of their basic religious tenets. Instead of inviting Christian "experts" to share what they knew about these different world religions, we asked actual representatives of these faiths to talk with us. Four Indian students represented Hinduism. Another evening a priest from the Chicago Buddhist temple came. A Muslim messenger issued a rather high-powered invitation. We felt the entire time had enhanced our appreciation of the thought patterns of our visitors from foreign lands. Later we were delighted by the presence of Father Mike Murphy, a seminarian, who dialogued with us for three weeks on Catholicism.

Any church business, including the annual meeting and elections, is held in this time slot. Planning for discussion groups and for the home worship services is also scheduled for the evening time. Since beginning, our entire government system of the church has undergone reorganization, requiring each member to determine his gifts and then to register with one of several interest groups, called modules. Nine have formed and a given Sunday night is designated "Monthly Module Night," with all these ministry-oriented groups meeting in different homes.

Quite often something will be scheduled just for a specific group, such as the singles, who will plan the program to fit their needs. Recently just families came to the church office, then proceeded in a group to view the magnificent display of Christmas ornamentation along State Street in the Loop and to sing around the massive lighted tree in the Civic Plaza. We then returned to the office to partake of hot chocolate and to watch the small children decorate the tree with the Christmas ornaments they had made. The comment was that we needed to do it more.

Since our prayer emphasis takes place within local geographic groups, there is often a need stated for requests on a broader basis. We then plan an all-church prayer meeting for a Sunday night rather than during the week. In August the area prayer groups meet on Sunday nights to give one month with no midweek interference.

In contrast to the Pastor's Class where the minister is asked questions, we recently concluded three weeks of Sunday evening "Congregation Classes" when the staff was given opportunity to make inquiries. The multiple sessions that took place each evening proved a very valuable means of discovering what people were thinking in regard to the direction the church was moving.

At present, an all-church progressive dinner is being planned that will involve many homes and eventually end with an outdoor baptismal service. That means the "Sunday evening service" will begin shortly after the morning one finishes. This gives an idea of our continued flexibility and also the Catch-All nature of this evening hour.

"What do you do about visitors who come on Sunday evening expecting a service and find no one at the Union Hall?" is a normal question heard. To begin with, our non-Christian guests seldom attend except when regulars invite them, and the regulars know when the services are held. If we miss people from another congregation who happen by wanting a Circle Church change of pace, we find comfort in knowing that we still have accomplished our major purpose for the evening—servicing the needs of our supportive membership.

Remember the homemaker's closet? Company is not supposed to open it. Occasionally an unsuspecting guest might do just that, causing the woman to hang a sign on the knob which reads, "For Family Only." This is the case of our Sunday evening service. If calls come to the office asking for information, we invariably give them the details of the morning program and say, "The evening is reserved mostly for our members and regular attenders. Often we don't meet in the Union Hall at all but in the homes of our congregation. We recommend that you become acquainted with Circle Church through the morning services. Then if you wish you can participate more fully in the church during the evening time also."

The church is not a building. It does not function exclusively within the mortar and wood and plaster wherein it is so often encased, nor does it breathe solely when assembled at certain hours. The church is the body of Christ and it exists wherever we exist. Realizing this truth has helped to free us from many of the constraints which might otherwise have been binding. Using Sunday evening in the most practical manner to service our members has helped to cut us loose and, as wise stewards, to guard the hours of time which fill the following week.

A Time to Pray

Surprisingly, it was to our advantage that the Union Hall was not available to us on weekdays. Consequently we were forced to schedule our prayer times in small home groups. These originally met once a month and were plotted according to geographic areas —if you happened to live on the south side of the city it was your turn when third Wednesdays came around. Although anyone from the church was welcome at all of the groups, the average area prayer meeting drew a steady core of attenders.

An interesting development has taken place in the last year. Several of the groups have voted to meet twice a month. If you miss one meeting, they say, it can be almost two months before you repeat the intense experience of sharing together. Now the majority of prayer groups meet at this rate. After a while some may want to revert back to once-a-month attendance or perhaps to increase to every week. That decision will be left to the pleasure of the individual prayer cell, the key word again being flexibility.

Admittedly, from the beginning these meetings have experienced tough going. Not only is prayer hard work, but many of the congregation had reluctant carry-overs from the past. They had no desire to participate again in the repetitious generalizations, the powerless "Hours of Power," the impersonal requests. Few, for that matter, had experienced vital private interceding, knowing little first-hand demonstrations of God's power. Nevertheless, we began meeting in small groups, having determined some basic prerequisites.

For one, the prayer requests were to be personal—what is **my** present need, at what point am **I** struggling? Although we entertained requests about individuals outside the circle, we strained to make our prayers center around the person we knew who was a part of us. "Let's see, I don't know your sister; and although I'm willing to pray that she will become warm to Christianity, I think I'm also going to remember you and the role you must play in her life."

Another prerequisite demanded that we be honest and not try to hide behind façades. If experiencing depression, we should state it; if joy, then that. The last requirement concerned mechanics. The time was not to be occupied by lecture— i.e., midweek Bible study —it was a **prayer** meeting. The method of prayer we preferred was conversational.

The advantage of meeting in homes was immediately recognized because a closeness developed that would not have been possible in a larger setting. There is something inherently warm and personal about houses in comparison with a church auditorium.

In time the groups began to hold their own, and the total monthly attenders represented a satisfactory percentage of the membership. Because the staff experiences personally the dynamic sustenance of these hours, we continue to emphasize participation on this level as being of utmost importance to spiritual development, and well worth the discipline required to attend. The groups are now functioning more and more smoothly, and because of the increase in their meeting times and the limitations on the part of staff members, they often have to continue without our direction. Although they do very well on their own, it is distinctly to our benefit to attend as many as possible, because it is here the heart of the congregation is most openly bared. It is here we are seeing tremendous Christian activity as victories are being won and God continues to meet needs.

When a person arrives at the meeting, he is given a 3" by 5" card on which to record each need. This way the praying doesn't have to cease after the evening together because people have forgotten the requests. Every once in a while there are so many requests that we don't have time for extended prayer. This is not necessarily bad, as we feel that God has been present listening to all that was said—He does not need the thoughts repeated to Him. Possibly the basic function of prayer on a small group level relates most closely to the bearing of one another's burdens, to concern and love freely given, and to the specific articulation of those needs to God, both that evening and in the days that follow.

Achieving an attitude which demands specific requests is what is desired. In fact, the groups are death on vagueness. Conversations which go as follows are quite familiar:

"Please pray for my unsaved neighbor."

"What do you want us to pray?"

"Well, pray that he will become a Christian."

Discussion usually follows as to whether it is legitimate to require God to impose Himself like a great clamp on the free will of that neighbor. Finally someone might respond, "Maybe what we ought to pray is that you will be able to relate your faith in a meaningful way to your neighbor."

Another may add, "I think I can pray for your neighbor, but in a specific sense; that God will prepare him through circumstances to be open to whatever you feel you can say to him."

Gently and kindly someone might then ask, "Why do you think it is that you haven't tried to relate to your neighbor until now?" and a short helpful dialogue may follow where ideas are expressed and reasons for reluctance are shared.

These conversations are not abnormal. We are anxious to make legitimate requests of God, and not to treat Him like a magic genie who must respond to our wish when the lamp is rubbed. God is not at our command, and we try to remind ourselves to pray in His interest.

We also attempt to keep our requests specific because it is so easy to hide human need behind generalities. It is hard for many of us to admit failure or to express shortcomings. It is equally difficult for a group to dig such feelings out of the individual before them. This demands a certain kind of courage, an obstinance which states, "We will not let you remain faceless before us. We're prodding and poking and pulling so that we can understand you, and share your life, both highs and lows, and ultimately love you." Often the honesty in a group will be paced by that of the leader, be he minister or layman.

One of the pastoral interns assigned to Circle Church from a nearby seminary had been asked to lead a prayer cell and had difficulty in drawing honesty from those present. The evening seemed to be dealing with superficialities. Finally it was my turn to make a request. I shared how I had allowed my schedule to grow too full and was now suffering because I hadn't experienced a completely satisfying time alone with God for quite awhile. I asked for prayer that I might soon straighten out my priorities. The group adjusted and the remaining requests were quite personal.

Afterwards the intern admitted to sweating out the unnaturalness of the first part. He asked what had precipitated the change. I explained that when any of us are confronted with authoritative strength, we are reluctant to expose ourselves. On the other hand all of us respond to weakness, either by being willing to share our own insufficiencies or to reach out to that one needing help. If at the first he had made his own request on the level of his personal needs, almost everyone in the group would have readily responded in like manner.

A sample of requests which have been shared in the groups within the last few weeks will help to illustrate their predominantly honest and specific qualities.

"I am still having trouble with drink. Please remember me."

"Pray that I may learn to overcome the little things in life which seem to irritate."

"There is going to be a change in our relationship because my husband is finishing school. Pray that we may help one another to make the necessary adjustments."

"My fiancé is going to the mission field, and I have great difficulty with my mental image of what missionaries are like. I don't want to conform my individuality in Christ, which I am just beginning to appreciate, to a mold which I feel is unworthy. Pray that I'll have wisdom to work out this dilemma."

"I'm still overweight. Pray that I will be open to God's reminding me of my need everytime I sit down to eat."

"I feel as though I have never used my talents for God as He would want, and yet I am a little confused as to what they are. Pray that God will give me understanding as to the several small areas I have in mind now and help me to move forward in playing my part in His kingdom."

"I have been procrastinating about writing an article that God has laid on my heart, and I just can't seem to get around to it. I guess I need self-discipline."

"I have established a pattern in my life where I always run from involvements once they begin to mean any kind of responsibility on my part. I need just once to stick with something I have begun."

"I am still not satisfied with being single and have not found peace that God intends me to remain this way. Pray that I may have His partner for me."

Such requests are rarely shared in a traditional prayer meeting. We can remember missionaries around the world and not know about the woman sitting next to us whose heart is breaking because a husband is being unfaithful. Where does she go for spiritual help, for burden-bearing, for counsel? The large auditorium or church basement, the seating arrangement of turning our backs to one another, the limited time because half of the precious moments have been devoted to another lecture (the third one of the week), all conspire against establishing a warm, trusting relationship. Even in churches where occasionally the practice of breaking into smaller groups is maintained, the principle of the stable situation is not perpetuated, because the same people are not in the divided groups week after week.

When I participate in seminars, I am usually asked, "Is it not quite risky to have such requests shared? There is always the problem of people within the church gossiping about what has been said." When everyone is open with one another, and nothing is hidden, there is no opportunity for gossip. Also, true Christians respond to weakness which has been openly expressed. A very thin line of distinction exists here, and it is basically the reason we ask that the requests be personal. A comment such as, "I know that so and so are having a difficult time in their marriage. I wish that you would pray . . ." might bring on a mental response of "Tsk, tsk, is that so? I never would have thought that possible. Why they seem to be such a happy pair." But when the couple themselves in an atmosphere of openness, share the conflicts of their marital situation, ask for prayer that they might know how to improve their attitude and consequently their marriage, the response of Christians seems to be one of genuine concern. Particularly is this so when each member of the group has been honest. When you have bared your soul, you will not take lightly the corresponding act of a fellow believer. In the entire experience of the prayer cells, I cannot think of one incident when this privilege of openness has been abused.

Recently my wife Karen noticed that I was exaggerating my facts slightly. In conversation the numbers became a little larger, the facts a little less factual. She commented on it—sweetly. I denied it—sweetly.

From that point on I began to hear nuances such as, "There, David, you just did it again." "See what I mean. That's not the way it happened." Finally the simple raising of an eyebrow convinced me her observation had been accurate.

This might seem like a little matter to some, but I have had past (and somewhat brutal) experience with fellow ministers who so stretched statements that they were no longer able to distinguish between truth and untruth. This all occurred at a time when I was undergoing distinct personal pressure, and we analyzed it as a symptom of those difficulties—compensation for some of the insufficiencies I was being made to feel.

I shared this problem with a prayer group. Now there are not many pastors who would feel free to state that they were having difficulties with lying. But I did, basically because I anticipated the group response to be, "David feels keenly about this and we will back him in prayer and do all we can to be of help." If I cannot, within the church, share my needs and have the people pray without gossiping about them, the sickness in the body is grave indeed.

When we discipline ourselves to give precise requests to God, we do ourselves an unexpected favor. It is easier to identify His supply when we pray specifically. How do we know if God has "blessed Agatha"? If Agatha has a wretched temper and needs help to control it and we all pray to that end, not only will Agatha be aware of the improvement, but the group will also—especially if its members have been continually affected by its meanness.

We have come therefore to expect answers to specific prayer. This is illustrated by the request that came from a factory foreman, Al Dines. He had experienced trouble with several employees, and asked for patience to work with them as a Christian should.

"Do you really mean that?" someone queried.

Yes he did.

"Well do you know what 'worketh patience'?"

Reluctantly he answered, "Tribulation."

Then the group decided that if we really expected God to create an attitude of patience in Al's life, we might as well pray for tribulation, since that was what produced it. Four weeks later at our next meeting, Al begged us to turn off the tribulation prayers because it had been the worst time he had ever put in at the factory.

"Have you learned patience?" someone asked.

"No."

"Do you want to still?"

"Yes," he sighed.

And we continued our prayers.

The next month Al reported that God **was** beginning to work a miracle of attitude within his life.

The number of times I have had someone ask, "Have you had an answer to that request you gave last week?" would be impossible to enumerate. This is true throughout the congregation. Our prayers are often answered by individuals pitching in when a need is expressed. If someone has been feeling weak, others minister to him. If a person has been lonely, others try to make introductions or extend dinner invitations to alleviate such a problem. If someone is having trouble with a given habit, he is sure to be asked again and again as the days proceed how he is doing, if he is overcoming. In fact, just knowing that people are going to check on your progress is incentive enough to overcome a fault, or to work on improvement, or to excel.

This is not to say that we don't experience God's hand separately from human initiative. Once while driving to the far northwest area prayer group, I was trying to pinpoint a specific request. Because I am in the groups so often, and because of the constant staff interaction, I may run out of requests! On this particular occasion I felt that God had done so much in my life I hardly knew what further to ask of Him. Yet, the more I traveled the more I remembered the physical tiredness I had experienced and decided that probably it was time for a vacation. Our vacations have consisted of speaking at Bible conferences and camps, which provided a change for Karen and the children but was draining for me. What I really needed was to get away for just a short period of time, with a minimum of meetings to cover the cost. That would be perfect!

After sharing all this with the group, I distinctly remember one of the ladies saying, "It's going to be interesting, David, to see how God answers this one." The following morning I had no sooner arrived in the office than a call came from a church in Florida saying, "Why don't you and Karen fly down, take several days just to enjoy yourselves, speak to us on Sunday and conduct a few seminars." Needless to say I was overwhelmed! Don and Norma Dutter from the church volunteered to stay with our kids (I think they knew why God had included Karen in the invitation by the time we returned), and the trip proved to be delightful beyond our expectations!

Everyone who has committed himself to participation in the prayer cells on an extended basis can testify to answered prayer. The enthusiasm engendered by this factor motivates us further to seek answers from God which are beyond our human means to provide.

The format of the prayer group from week to week can be quite different. We usually begin with something that will set a mood for sharing. Perhaps we mention areas in which we can give thanks to God, or perhaps we will take time to praise Him with each person contributing. Individuals may want to give a testimony. It could be that everyone answers the question, "How am I doing spiritually?" Once as we shared requests, we stretched our minds to ask, "To which attribute of God does this request pertain?" We may take time to read a portion of Scripture. A large part is given to catching up on the progress of the requests from the previous meetings and to redefining additional needs. For actual prayer we may stay together in the large group, or we may break into smaller cells of three to four people.

Following the prayer time, the hostess will usually prepare refreshments. When we first started the groups, we stipulated that refreshments were not to be served. But they seem to be an inevitable thing. I think we have come past the point where each woman tries to outdo the one before her. In fact, at the last meeting at our house, Karen served apples, popcorn, and orange juice— which happened to be the only suitable things we had on hand.

This generation is anti-cliché. It is continually searching for fresh and vital ways to express its faith. The word "blessing" has been unofficially banned at Circle because of its ambiguity, and we make an attempt to express our prayer in everyday, understandable language rather than reverting to flowery, mini-liturgical phrases. Our purpose is not to impress the group, but to communicate with God, and we do it in the way which is most familiar, personal and useful.

The group prays conversationally. This has basically eliminated the speechmaking which otherwise often occurs. Each individual limits his comments to the maximum time of one minute. The others respond as we feel inclined, just as we would in any other conversation, except that this one is addressed to God. It goes something like this:

Cathy: Father, we pray for Alex who has stated a need for physical strength especially in the face of exams which are coming up.

Don: Father, thank you that he has gotten over his bout with the flu. Now help the healing process to continue.

Bob: Help him to realize he can't waste his limited strength and expect you to undertake his cause.

Cathy: Give him the discipline to turn off the TV and go to bed.

George: Father, I just want to thank you for the way you've helped me in this very area of self-discipline. I feel like I've grown so much and am really improving. Thank you.

Darrel: I pray for the group at Elmhurst College as they prepare this rock festival as an evangelistic means for reaching students on the campus.

Bob: Help the group to be controlled so that there is no rowdiness.

Cathy: Also move in the hearts of church members around the area to respond to the need for sandwiches.

This conversational method provides for tremendous spontaneity and freshness. It is not unusual for the group during prayer to laugh together, a marvelous comment on the unstilted, natural progress of our prayer life.

Being time conscious (as usual) at first I felt that the groups shouldn't go any longer than an hour. I am learning to relax now, and if certain ones want to be together longer after refreshments are served, I'm certainly not going to get nervous about that, as long as the hostess doesn't. It's not unusual for the groups to continue from 7:30 until 10:30 or 11:00.

What have we learned through the prayer cells? Well, a great deal about being honest, about expecting God to answer us, about sharing, about responding to need. We are learning that to be involved together makes it seem natural to call one another any time through the week and ask to be remembered regarding a matter. We are learning that, with the assistance of a group, we can step out on the thin edge of faith. We are learning about simplicity of expression, about acceptance. In short, in our prayer groups, we are learning about prayer!

III.

COMING FULL CIRCLE

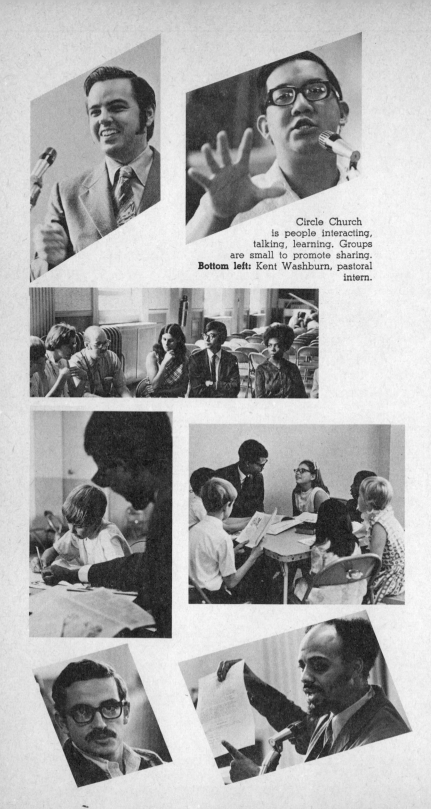

Circle Church
is people interacting,
talking, learning. Groups
are small to promote sharing.
Bottom left: Kent Washburn, pastoral
intern.

Chapter Six

"We're marching to Zion,
Beautiful, beautiful Zion."

Approaching the end of the school year in June of 1968, we were almost a year and a half old, and our attendance hovered constantly around the two hundred mark. With the remarkable enthusiasm present, we projected that it was quite feasible we would pass three hundred by the end of September, which was alarming because we had a "number hang-up." Now most church staffs want to lift off the roof, shoot for the sky, break last year's attendance record. But we had committed ourselves to a small church philosophy because it seemed more adequately to facilitate intense interaction. Two hundred was the magic number beyond which we predicted the bond of person-to-person fellowship would be stretched unbearably. In anticipation of this, we had decided previously that we would either begin a branch work or split off part of the group to infuse new life into a dying city congregation.

Seeing that the determined point had been reached, we began making overtures in various directions. Several possibilities were explored. (1) Maybe there were leftover buildings vacated by extinct congregations. We found, however, that none were free for the asking. (2) We investigated establishing a branch work, but the undertaking of financing even a minimal staff seemed prohibitive. (3) We contacted the District Superintendent to inquire whether any churches within our own denomination, the Evangelical Free Church, would welcome our assistance. There were three. Two exist to this day without our help. The last died with our help! Its name was the Zion Evangelical Free Church.

Zion Church was located in the explosive Austin area of the city which is racially altering and was at this time deeply embroiled

135

in conflicts stemming from the busing of school children. In a period of three to four years the church had dropped from an average membership of three hundred fifty to a dismal thirty, as members regularly exited to the suburbs.

It is difficult even now to describe adequately the events which took place in our disjointed union, since the emotions, personalities, and relationships involved tend to color clear thinking. In many ways we are still feeling the whiplash of crashing into failure. Because of the drastic outcome of this venture we have examined our motives to see if they were as honorable as we thought they were. Personally, and I speak for the rest of the membership, I was not trying to build a huge kingdom of my own (e.g., one of the nation's ten largest Sunday schools). In fact, I was studiously avoiding it. My heart yearned for the city and I longed to see Christ walk its concrete canyons. How better could this be effected than by seeing His church experience renaissance—lights coming alive in neighborhoods citywide? We were willing to forego a powerhouse base of our own, if we could only play a role in this overall renewal.

In order to contrast the two organizations it will be necessary to examine the psychology of the Circle Church body at that time and to illustrate it from personal experience. We will probably never again match the height of enthusiasm which we were then experiencing as a whole. We may accomplish more significant things, but we will never regain that purity in which the high spirits of the individual matched that of the total core. We were like a people under siege, united by the most basic cause—survival.

Even more so we shared a dream, a Camelot. We had jointly walked to the edge of our resources and cast ourselves forth in a venture which would survive only if God would undertake. Our faith had been returned, "pressed down, and shaken together, and running over. . . ." We daily experienced the miraculous. We felt that our dream, this experiment which essentially dealt with church renewal, had been vindicated by God in the intense spiritual growth we shared, in conversions, and in the maintenance of our basic material needs. Corporately we had encountered two years of spiritual high.

On a personal level Karen and I rediscovered Christianity in its elemental form—learning that the truths imparted in early training had application. "Company's coming!" was the first sentence our daughter Melissa spoke, and company certainly did come! It was open house every day. The table could be set for breakfast, lunch, or dinner, and we can't recall how many times we weren't sure we would have food to put on the plates. We followed literally Christ's commandment, "Don't worry about **things**—food, drink, and clothes. . . . Your Heavenly Father already knows perfectly well that you need them. And He will give them to you gladly if you put Him first in your life" (Matt. 6:25, 31, Taylor). We were blatant "grasshoppers," never storing for tomorrow, yet God's promise **always** held true.

Paychecks were often two weeks or more overdue, near disaster for people with no padding, no savings account, no stocks or bonds to cash in, nothing set aside for a rainy day. I'm not saying that we didn't eat a lot of eggs and meatless meals, or that we didn't execute royal hunts through drawers, and pockets, and upholstered pieces for loose change to pay bus fares or luncheon appointments. (My mother would often demand, "David, why do you let Karen go out without any money?" The simple reason was that there was no money to give her.)

What I am saying is there was no sense of privation or sacrifice, because God's mercy was abundant. There was adequate provision for our needs, and always enough when we extended ourselves in the ministry of hospitality. Two brown paper bags of day-old bakery goods found their way to our door every Sunday, compliments of faithful friends from the church of our former employment. With their contents we made sandwiches, served desserts, provided rolls and coffee for group meetings, had the basics to share morning meals with overnight guests, and for three years never bought a loaf of bread. Often we invited people for breakfast because that was the only kind of food available. Eggs and bacon, sweet rolls and juice stretched a long way.

Inevitably, when we had literally spent our last penny, a check would arrive in the mail bearing payment for an article we had written. It never came when we were in the black, but always in time to keep us from going into the red. Sacks of vegetables from my father-in-law's farm kept us healthy in the summer, and we usually had enough tomatoes to share with our neighbors. For several months a money order regularly arrived from Missouri and supplied our needs during a particularly touch-and-go time, and though it was unsigned, we were aware of the donor. (Thank you, Cindy.)

Karen combed resale shops and Salvation Army stores with great relish, and her eye for fine antiques and for form and design transformed what I viewed as "junk" into the makings of a warm and comfortable home. In fact she became so proficient at refinishing and restoring these odd objects that she was asked to give lectures to women's groups. Consequently, payment for her topic, "The Art of Junking," was another means that helped us through the tight spots. She never said "No" to hand-me-downs, and between secondhand clothes and the sewing machine was able to assemble an attractive wardrobe for herself and the children. The basic attitude she maintained was that everything we had, from the Victorian chair she had reupholstered to the oak bunk beds salvaged from someone's moving discard, came from God's hand and to Him we were grateful.

One of the most interesting developments of this time was the attitude of our neighbors toward us. Every pastor and his family has had to endure certain misconceptions. In fact, we suspect one couple actually moved from next door because the tension of maintaining a role in our presence was uncomfortable. But I think we came to be viewed as one of the local phenomenon, along with the hippies and night spots and wax museum.

It was impossible for our neighbors to miss the significance of one group of visitors following on the heels of another—their different races, the international flavor, the Catholic priest who visited and stayed overnight. They were aware of our high spirits as the sounds of our hilarity floated through open windows (even in winter because the apartment overheated) and into the common halls. They observed us getting along together without the stimulation of drugs or alcohol, observed through the uncurtained windows which faced each other across the courtyard the same group praying. (The courtyard atmosphere was uninhibited to say the least. Often while sitting in our living room I would view a neighbor cross a room clad in undershirt and shorts only to have him smile and wave!)

We began to experience what it meant to be "a light in the

world," and to participate in those rather heady moments of knowing that the Holy Spirit has prepared the way as you speak naturally about Christ in the most unlikely of surroundings. We found ourselves to be an influence and an example for good. We invited the crankiest neighbor for dinner, managed to provide a roast, listened to him expound for hours about his fascinating background, allowed him to unload his gnawing bitterness, and discovered to our amazement that from that point not only did we no longer have trouble with him, but neither did the rest of the courtyard!

It was easy to share faith out of the exuberance of our feelings. "What a darling dress!" someone would exclaim to Karen.

"Thank you. Like I always say, God has great taste!" she would reply referring to the outfit that was invariably a hand-me-down.

"I found two sacks with 'Mains' written on them by our door. Must be yours."

"Oh, thank goodness. That's our manna. I'm glad you found them. I think I have people coming for breakfast tomorrow. Without those sacks, Mother Hubbard's cupboard is definitely bare!" (A discussion about God's providing daily bread naturally followed.)

We found ourselves in the unusual position of being ministered to by the unchurched neighbors in our community.

"I baked some brownies for your Board meeting tonight."

"Let me know if I can take the children to the zoo with us today. Then you'll have time to get ready for your company."

"If the baby comes when you're not around, Reverend, have your wife call the store. We'll use the delivery wagon to drive her to the hospital."

"Take these flowers home to your wife. Ah! Don't bother to pay me for them. They're a day old. They'll wilt soon." So the gifts from our Greek florist filled centerpieces and pitchers in our home. (I had given him a copy of Billy Graham's "Peace with God" in response to a conversation we had had, and he reciprocated in full.)

My barber, Buster, came to church with us. "We prefer to buy experiences rather than things," commented one friend who was deeply interested in Zen. "I can see your philosophy is the same." Unknown to her we **were** making rather heavy investments—not on the earthly level though. I visited the grocery store checkout lady in the hospital as she lay dying of cancer and led her to the Lord, then was asked by the family to conduct the funeral. "Such a change came in Mom the last months after you talked with her." Our lives were positively bound with our community in the city!

It was with these marvelous experiences, these feelings of exuberance and power, this sense of invincibility because we had seen God meet our dependence time and again, that we entered into the union with the Zion Evangelical Free Church. Usually when a city church is dying the others wait like vultures to pick up some of the survivors. We were doing the unusual. We were going to send people to keep it alive for Christ.

Negotiations went on for several months between our two groups, and the more we examined one another, the more convinced we each became that an arrangement was the answer to our separate dilemmas. Circle needed a place to direct its energetic growth and Zion needed a transfusion of new blood. Whereas they had recently called three men to the pulpit with unsuccessful results, we thought that we could guarantee a consulting pastor from our group. We were always low on funds, but they had a savings account with several thousand dollars which they readily agreed could be put toward paying his salary. We were mostly young and they were mostly old. We felt we could benefit from cooperation with a different age group and they wanted very much to have their church filled with young people again. We had a philosophy of change which we thought needed to be tested in a traditional situation, and they felt change was necessary to reach the new environment which existed in their neighborhood. In short, it was a ready-made situation.

After much prayer on both sides, we "knew" God was definitely in the plan.

A contractual agreement was drawn up and sailed through both congregations. The essential outline consisted of these points:

1. A short explanation of the "Circle Approach" emphasized its genesis stemming from dissatisfaction with the organized church which we found not facing the issues of the day, a church not supplying relevant answers, a church not relating to modern man living in an ever-changing and technologically complex world, a church that was basically ingrown. The agreement then went on to state, "The

'Circle Approach' says that members should not be involved in endless programs, but rather in the ministry of the church in their respective worlds. They should gather for worship, prayer, and discussion in order to build and strengthen each other in the faith, so they may better share that faith in their individual daily lives."

2. SERVICES TO BE RENDERED

"For a period of one year commencing on September 1, 1968, and continuing through and including August 31, 1969, Circle shall furnish Zion the services of a full-time consulting minister, a part-time minister of music, and a pulpit minister for each Sunday morning service. The consulting minister, under the direction and guidance of Circle staff, shall work directly with the Zion congregation. In this capacity he shall analyze Zion's needs and potential in order that a church ministry based on the 'Circle Approach' will be developed and implemented in Zion's congregational and community ministry. The minister of music, also under the direction and guidance of Circle staff, shall develop and implement a church music program which will complement the work of the consulting minister. The obligation for Circle to provide a pulpit minister for Sunday morning services will generally be fulfilled by the consulting minister assigned to Zion by Circle. However, it is understood that Circle will use its entire pastoral staff as well as laymen from both congregations to fulfill this part of its obligations."

3. PAYMENT FOR SERVICES

At this point a pay scale was determined covering salaries, travel and hospitality, medical insurance, housing costs, and office expenses. Circle agreed to keep separate books of all expenditures made from Zion funds and at the expiration of the agreement, or at any time requested, to furnish Zion a statement in writing summarizing all such expenditures and to return unspent funds at the termination of the agreement.

4. NON-TERMINABLE AGREEMENT

We jointly agreed to bind ourselves to the agreement for the period of one year, with the only exception being "if Zion should determine it has unreconcilable disagreements with the consulting minister on spiritual matters or on the implementation of the 'Circle Approach' to Zion's congregational and community ministry, then Zion shall

notify Circle's Board of Deacons in writing of such disagreements, and request that a different consulting minister be assigned to Zion." The contract stipulated that such
action on Zion's part should have prior approval of no less
than a two-thirds majority of its then existing church membership.

5. AUTONOMY OF ZION AND CIRCLE
"It is acknowledged that both Zion and Circle are presently
independent autonomous church organizations and that it
is not the intent of this agreement to alter or affect the complete autonomy of either organization. Each retains the
right to govern itself completely independent of the other
in any manner whatsoever as established by its respective
congregational membership."

With the signatures on the bottom of that contract we bound ourselves to a one year experiment with Zion which began on September 1, 1968, with a young member of our congregation, Al
Nestor, acting as consulting minister. Al's previous experience had
been with Chicagoland Youth for Christ, and he had been most
effective in his assignment as a youth worker. His territory had
covered the near west suburbs and the very Austin area in which
Zion church was located. He had become active at Circle to the
point of preaching during a morning service, and I had great confidence in him as a person. His wife Lynn was an extremely attractive girl and in every way fitted to be a help to her husband.
They were both in their early twenties.

It was by coincidence, in a way, that Al went to Zion. As we
began the Zion negotiations, Al underwent a job change, and his
future became a question mark, with further schooling looming as
a possibility. In discussions of likely candidates to take the Zion
responsibility, Al's name was mentioned again and again. One of
his valuable qualities was his optimism, a quality we felt was
imperative for whoever would try to make a go of the effort. Al
seemed as caught up with the whole idea as the rest of us, and it
wasn't long before he and Lynn had committed themselves to the
one-year period agreed upon in the contract. We determined that
he would preach three Sundays out of five at Zion as I did at Circle,
and the rest of the staff would pulpit-supply other Sundays, although Al would always be present at Zion unless used to preach
at Circle to give reports of what was taking place.

I don't see how things could have gone better—for the first month! It seemed to be that kind of romance where neither group saw the other's fault. From my files I have included a letter that was sent out by Al at the beginning of October which demonstrates the feeling that everyone had.

It has been exactly one month since I accepted the responsibility as pastor of Zion Church. A church with forty-eight years of experience had nearly died. Attendance had never been lower. Three pastors had decided to decline invitation to this pulpit within the year. In one month things have changed.

Let me illustrate with comments from three men. One board member had been praying for his dying church for years. He feels God has now answered his prayers. He is open to the various changes being made at Zion and in his exuberance even made the comparison of these innovations with those brought about by Martin Luther! A second man had attended for two years to encourage the people since the first sentiment was expressed favoring closing Zion Church. He now reminds the people that other urban churches are carefully observing what is happening here. A third man led his first Bible discussion group . . . probably had never been asked before. After a thorough study and assistance from the library, he did a tremendous job. He is an integral part of God's plan for Zion.

As pastor, I am trying to seek purpose in every activity. This church will be a **group effort** involving **every** interested person. God through His Spirit is developing each individual as we work together. That is part of the reason that the average attendance has more than doubled in one month.

It was quite fascinating to see the attendance boom, and there were several Sundays when it actually went over 100. Some of the people at Zion had tears in their eyes because they hadn't seen this many people out for a good while.

Then the cold hard light of reality began to dawn. We were aware, of course, that a few individuals at Zion had expressed disfavor with the arrangement. The best giver in the congregation, for example, was reported to have left during the negotiations as soon as he heard blacks would be welcome. The rumors began to float, bit by bit, in all directions. We saw in disconnected flashes what were to be the irreconcilable differences of the groups. Some of them were the very things which had made us attractive to one another.

Circle people were basically optimistic, while the Zion remnant was justifiably defeated. They were nursing the wounds of a church split which had embittered many of them years before, and they had been part of the disheartening dwindling of a local church. Many of our young congregation had sought to shake off the emphasis of their upbringing, that preoccupation with externalism, the market list of "Don't! Don't! Don't!" by which spirituality was wrongly determined. Many of the Zion people, on the other hand, had no other basis for judging faith. This conflict culminated in a reaction to mini skirts, and one family left the church because of the long sideburns of the new songleader.

We were ridiculously young, with all the basic characteristics of that age group—vigor, a desire to move ahead, idealism, restless energy for world-changing, confidence in our innate abilities. The majority of Zion people were senior citizens, retirees who were not filled with zestful enthusiasm but were adapting themselves to the impositions of old age and limited incomes. Many were reactionary, holding to the good times which had once been meaningful. Many clung to the shreds of a once-familiar world which had gone awry —the most secure place being the church which had sustained them through the years, the place where they had brought their children for training and baptism, the comfortable climate of the church womb.

The first source of dissatisfaction on the part of the Zion people stemmed from the fact that Circle people didn't return after visiting one or two times. "Where are all the people you promised us?" they demanded. I will not claim that a huge group of Circle regulars changed their support to Zion, but an adequate, if not elite, group did.

The way was led by our Board Chairman, Bill Weiss and his family, then a producer and announcer at radio station WMBI. Several couples, one a clinical marriage counselor, one a student at Northwestern University, another a student from India and his beautiful Afro-American wife, made the move. Our former church secretary, her husband, and their new baby became Zionites. Of course there were Al and Lynn Nestor. The music program was eventually headed by Steve Bell who had toured with Venture for

Victory in the Orient the summer before. He and his fiancée
Valerie, a voice major, were studying at Moody Bible Institute.
Several singles, mostly in the student status, attended regularly
and pitched in to help with the music and education programs.

The number was not as large as either group had hoped for.
Zion people could not help but hold what they felt was our defi-
ciency against us. What we hadn't counted on was the tremendous
pull into the past that Zion church exerted on so many of our congregation. The name itself, the building, the fastened church pews,
the off-key organ were all symbolic of things so many of our young
people had rejected and were determined not to submit to again.
Some of them had only recently come to terms with their faith,
and much of that struggle had been realized within the openness
and sharing of Circle. Many had freed themselves of the child of
their past and admitted that they were not ready to participate in
the major effort of pulling Zion to its feet. Some came to me and
said, "Dave, I would give anything if I were big enough to help
out. But I just can't. I'm not ready to go back into that type of
situation again." It was a fight against psychological reactions
which had been completely unanticipated.

Although we had stressed that Circle people would need a certain amount of "courting," we had also not anticipated the inability
of the Zion regulars to provide sociability on levels to make the
transfusion group feel welcome. If hospitality has not been extended during the course of a lifetime, it is not easy all of a sudden
to welcome strangers, and very young ones at that, into your home.
Making conversation in a way which draws response is a practiced
art and definitely requires effort. If you have not forced yourself
continually to reach out from comfortable in-groups through the
years of aging, it is more than difficult to begin such activity late
in life.

So we reached an impasse of sorts. Our people who attended
several times with a subdued willingness to participate found the
hesitant efforts of welcome in startling contrast to the warm
gregarious atmosphere we had worked so hard to establish at
Circle. On the other hand, Zion people, who were basically an
older, more reserved group, and had known one another for years
and years, were unable to assimilate these newcomers with their
short, short skirts and lists of degrees.

The methods employed on Sunday morning during the service also made for difficulties. Zion people had never heard several people pray at the same time, nor Scripture being read from different points in the congregation rather than being intoned from the platform. The choir was moved from the front of the auditorium—where the congregation could see every nose blow, every purse searched, every head that bobbed in sleep—to the balcony in back. Using recordings in place of special music was a dangerous innovation to many. These conceptual dilemmas were symbolic of the whole confrontation—the difficulty of mixing the new with the old, current styles with familiar and much-loved traditions, reaching out with pulling in.

From our vantage point, there was a continual temptation to criticize what we interpreted as narrowness and small-mindedness without struggling for the grace to try to understand the background of experience that limited so many of those people. Later, after we had gone through the Zion year, we realized that if we could not look at our role and ask, "What did we do wrong? What areas did we push which were not important? How could we have approached it differently?" and then uproot satisfying answers to these questions—if we could not force ourselves to do this as opposed to blame-finding, and finger-pointing, and judgmental attitudes, then the whole effort had been useless. We would have learned nothing about ourselves and our limitations. The experiment would then have been a failure in the ultimate sense.

Using our new methodology in the Service of Worship and Instruction was an area in which we feel we made a real mistake. As Al pointed out later, "To so many of the Zion people, this service was their one point of continuity in a drastically altered world which they found difficult to comprehend and of which many were afraid. To come Sunday after Sunday and find things the same was reassuring. Suddenly that too was changed, radically for some." Although we had explained the philosophy, and had tried to interpret how it found its outworkings in methodology, and they had agreed to it, the actuality was hard for them to bear. I think if we had cautiously educated the group in our philosophy and its scriptural base, and had suited the methodology to Zion's individual personality rather than transplanting what had been done previously at Circle, we could have prevented much of the shock reaction which occurred. (But then, of course, even fewer Circle people would have stayed!)

October and November were months when small tremors rumbled through both congregations as to whether we could actually pull off the venture. This precipitated more prayer on the part of us all; as a Circle staff we spent hours encouraging one another. There were months when I put in almost as much time working on Zion with Al as I did with Circle. I felt that our whole philosophy was at stake. The days fluctuated between a feeling that we were going to see a real victory and one that nothing on earth could make it go.

Despite the damaging effects of mounting criticism, we saw some lovely examples of the triumph of the human spirit. Al's greatest trouble was accustoming his people to the concept that each had been given at least one gift of the Holy Spirit to be used for ministry in the community. It seemed to be foreign to them. For those who actually experimented with expressing what was locked inside there was delight and fulfillment. We were excited when a middle-aged man taught a discussion group. He had never spoken to a group before and, in fact, was so nervous about doing things in public that his wife would pray when dinner guests were present. Unsure about the new experience, he studied for hours every night. When the day finally arrived, he did an excellent job!

One elderly man who had been attending the church for twenty-three years was overwhelmed that **he** had been asked to serve communion. Maybe our attempt, in spite of its eventual demise, was validated by such small steps as these.

On the other hand, there were those who bucked the concept. Accustomed to previous ministers' making visitation calls, they could not understand why this was not a part of our pattern. Al explained that the minister's role was to help develop these gifts on the part of the laity. When visitation was necessary, in his role as the player-coach, Al would take men from the church with him in an attempt to teach them how to take over. Even though they had acquiesced when we had explained that developing the gifts of the Holy Spirit was a major foundation to our philosophy, the application which expected them to do their share of what the pastor was being paid to do was difficult to understand.

For Al there was no textbook available for a consulting source when he became enmeshed in these problems. He had to find out by doing. In my evaluation, for a young man facing tremendous problems with limited experience, he did a remarkable job. We spent hours together. I was grateful that God had blessed Al with a sense of humor, because he was able to laugh on many occasions when it might have been more appropriate to cry.

I remember the first Pastor's Class I conducted, in which I began by asking the people to tell who they were and give some background. "After all, it is hard to discuss if we don't know a little bit about one another." The first man was one of the members of the church Board. "My name is Richard, and I am a retired letter carrier." As he spoke, the wife of the Board chairman gasped, "I didn't know you were a mail man!"

We can never know everything about anyone, of course, and if this had been an isolated incident we could have accepted it. But more and more as people opened to one another in the discussion groups they discovered facts which should have come out in the previous years of church attendance. That Richard had been a letter carrier clearly revealed the basic elements of his livelihood. If these primary facts were not being communicated, how could they possibly expect complicated trials and needs and despairs to be freely shared. In a few months' time we were not having trouble motivating the older people to talk—only to stop talking! Many times I would stay past noon—until 12:30 or quarter to one— because people wanted to continue these interactions around the common element of their faith.

The Zion people were building-oriented. They had struggled to maintain it with such dedication that it was not unusual for Al and Lynn to come upon an individual cleaning the vestibule steps. There was no committee. In a beautiful way, each came spontaneously to do his part and without particularly wanting anyone else to know about his role. The auditorium had been painted recently, and when stained glass windows were broken by neighborhood children, the members patiently restored the pieces. Many of these people had helped to pay for that very building, and unconsciously it had become a shrine devoted to middle-class work ethics as well as having symbolic religious overtones. Consequently, the theory of the church in the marketplace, and a possible use of other gifts of the Spirit, was next to impossible for them to assume.

Moving the prayer group out of the austere basement room with
its connotations of "Midweek Service" and into the warm informal-
ity of homes which would be more conducive to personal sharing
was met with, "Why move? We've always done it this way!" The
solution was to make the church available as well as home groups.
Yet, it seemed impossible to initiate any psychology different from
the one which viewed the building as the focus of sociability and
spirituality.

Al called me after the Zion Board meeting in November to report
with pleasure the apparent progress. The spirit was good, and he
felt that many of the difficulties were being overcome. He said
there had been a request for him to leave at the end so they could
discuss one further matter of business. "What was that about?" I
asked. He didn't have any idea, possibly they were thinking of
a Christmas bonus for him.

"Hey, great!" I responded. Oh, woe unto us, the optimistic
dreamers of this world who lead with our chins!

It wasn't long before three key members of the Board called me
and requested a special meeting. They were very anxious that the
staff and people at Circle understand that they were displeased
with what was happening—this after a meeting with Al in which
they had given him the impression of good will. Obviously, the
displeasure had been voiced after he had been excused.

The key issue seemed to be money. Zion people were worried
as their several-thousand-dollar balance continued to shrink, and
they projected that by the end of the year it would all disappear.
We had experienced two years of total dependence on God in
which He had met every one of our needs. To talk about a bank
balance of several thousand dollars to a man who was grateful
for books which were $.47 in the black was an example of a com-
munications gap to say the least. I pointed out that the most
important thing to consider was whether or not God was working,
and quoted the Scripture which expressly forbids our being worried about tomorrow's needs. They had more than enough money
to meet their obligations for three or four more months. But they
were wrapped up in thoughts of the regular givers who had left
and by our failure to provide more Circle people.

They also wanted to make sure that the money was being used
exclusively for Zion needs. I assured them that separate books
were being kept, which they were welcome at any time to see,

and pointed out that although not as many people had changed churches as we had hoped, the ones who had thrown their shoulders to the wheel had also designated their tithes and offerings to the Zion funds with our blessing. Also, I hoped that in time other Circle folk would transfer. (In fact I stressed this so often in our own church, one key friend told me emphatically that I was making him feel so guilty, if I didn't stop he wouldn't come back to Circle!)

Yet the problems with the Zion Board were much deeper than material need. It was one of an ingrained attitude. The whole mental framework was defeatist. Everything they saw was a difficulty and not an opportunity. Whereas we were coming to observe problems with an attitude which said, "This is something we can overcome through the creative empowering of God's Spirit," they could respond only by grumbling and complaining. The few indications we had from them of an optimistic spirit were heartening, but there were very few.

As we examined carefully what they were saying, we realized that they had thought Circle Church would be the savior of the Zion situation. They had thought we would restore the church to its years of former glory, to an auditorium that was full again, a program packed with activities, where the peers were all white and all conformed to the image of one another. Since we all sift information through the background of our experience and expectations, I suppose both sides were guilty of interpreting the data of our contractual agreement as they saw fit. And I suppose Circle's healthy confidence in itself did nothing to dissuade them that we would not be able to do exactly what they dreamed of our doing.

But we were not able to restore their dream, and this was a discouraging matter to them. They were not able to fulfill our hopes, and this was a source of disappointment and impatience to us.

Eventually the men centered their complaints around their young minister. Possibly they had agreed beforehand to petition me about this, because it was an escape mechanism which had been provided for; our contractual agreement stipulated that they could request a different consulting pastor. They wanted that change now. They wanted Pastor Nestor sent back to Circle, and they wanted Pastor Mains to be their minister. Of course my defenses were all for Al. I had worked hours with him, and grown to love and respect him. I had watched with admiration the growth he had displayed and the overwhelming amount of love he had showered on this group of people. To have him so ill-treated was unbearable. (Al has since accused me of "losing my cool" in that meeting.)

Talking further, I explained some of the changes I would make if I came, the smallest of which was enough to strike terror in their hearts. I wouldn't be nearly as patient as Al had been (an example of which they were seeing now). They agreed that I wasn't their man. I then asked if they wanted our black pastor, and of course that represented problems right away.

"Well, how about Ka Tong Gaw?" Ka Tong had some months back vocally expressed his impatience with the complaints of this new congregation, enough to convince them that he wouldn't be right either.

It ended with their agreeing to try the experiment further under the direction of Pastor Nestor. In conclusion, I emphasized again Al's love for them and, naming each man, pointed out the specific ways in which he had clearly received that love.

The next months were trying. Still we often felt that if we just stuck with it long enough, prayed faithfully, and trusted God to work, we would turn a corner. Al took as his major theme the sufficiency of God's help. He wanted to impress the people with the fact that even if Circle hadn't come to offer assistance, with **God's** help they would be able to move forward and see their local body grow. Unfortunately the more effort we made, the more resistance we encountered; and the more resistance we encountered, the more of a tendency developed among the Circle people to remove themselves from the problem.

Finally the Circle Church Board met to decide whether to break the nonterminable agreement of our contract at the request of the Zion group. The discussion favored letting them go ahead with whatever they desired. I adamantly opposed this direction. "You realize, of course, everything we believe in goes down the drain when this happens. I don't see how we can vote this way."

As so often occurs, the Board went against me—and proved to be right. When it took the vote and by a margin of one decided to let the Zion people make the decision without our holding them to the total-year contract, I was upset.

"What do we have left?" was my reaction.

Jack Feldballe, (I play "Mutt" to his six-foot-six "Jeff") turned and said: "We have Christ left and He's all that really counts, David."

The contract could have ended, but to Zion's credit they continued under it the remaining eight months. In that time a key Zion Board member quit without warning, a man who had told Al to his face that he was very much behind him. Even his letter of resignation contained nothing but praise for Al, although he had expressed an opposite viewpoint to me. I don't know if a life style had rendered him incapable of honestly telling what he felt or if he really didn't know and floundered in indecision.

One way or other the August 31, 1969, ending of the contract resulted in a congregational vote to cease being a church. Zion died with profound implications for our own situation. I still have ambivalent feelings toward the experience—thrilled to be free of it and yet at the same time wondering if we had stuck with it, done it a little differently, would it have succeeded? We coped with failure and called it by name. **We had failed.** We tried to see where we had been grandiose, where cocky in our own strength, where presumptuous instead of faithful.

With hindsight we determined that one of our major problems had been an emphasis on methodology rather than a patient understanding of philosophy. The Zion people reacted against our methods, and complained that the Circle people didn't attend; and the Circle people were sold on the methods they had experienced before and didn't stay at Zion because there was no freedom on that point. It was one of the many cyclical routes we traveled.

After the Zion experience, our people and the staff were naturally reluctant to cope with an adventure of this kind again. Perhaps some day we would feel open to starting a work from scratch. Al came onto our staff part time. The growth at Circle continued, now without a willingness to siphon ourselves off in another direction. Licking our wounds we realized, rather Johnny-come-lately, that it is very difficult to change the traditional church, and there aren't going to be many who are open to new ideas, no matter how graciously they are presented.

Perhaps we should have been forewarned. The second time I preached at Zion Church, I used Psalm 23 for my text. At the very beginning of the sermon, an older gentleman who had not attended church for several years gave a loud groan and collapsed in his pew. An ambulance was called, but it was too late. He was dead. The experience was symbolic of the entire venture.

A close friend once pointed out to me one of the major faults of a physical church building. "Some churches ought to die," he said. "They have no vitality, no force, no virility. In essence they **are** dead. They maintain a semblance of life only because the church building stands. Without that, they would have died at the proper time and not been a blotch on the life-force which is supposed to represent Christianity."

Maybe Zion should have been allowed to die. Maybe we were like those medical technicians who sustain bodily functions in corpses. At any rate, I hoped that if ever the time came when **we** became sterile, no longer reproductive, we would have the courage and strength to die quickly, to close the books, to say, "It was glorious once, wasn't it?"

The greatest lesson we learned was that we cannot expect any place to be a carbon copy of Circle Church. We had made more changes in two years' time than had taken place in decades. It was only as that growth was juxtaposed against the background of Zion that we could evaluate its depth and intensity. It is impossible to think of having churches follow us down the same path. They could never begin where we presently are—it would be the ruination of many. They must wrestle with a philosophy of existence and then apply a methodology of their own.

One night some months later, Al was awakened by a phone call, "Pastor Al, Zion church is burning." At the scene of the fire, Al watched as this building, beloved of many, empty now of all life, went up in flames. Then he noticed a church member, Doc, whose wife had died recently, and they began to talk. At the end of the conversation Doc whispered, "Well, Pastor Al, we almost pulled it off, didn't we?"

The poet Dylan Thomas once enjoined his father, "Do not go gentle into that good night." Perhaps those are my sentiments. Despite the agony and the frustration, despite the wrenching and the discouragement, it was better not to go gently into the good night of oblivion. It was better to rage and pull and fight and press on, to climb and strive and stretch, than to sink helplessly into morbidity, into senility, into comatosity, into uselessness.

We had fought a good fight. We had lost.

Chapter Seven

God and Mr. Peick weren't through.

By the end of the summer of 1969 we were behind financially and had received notice to move from the downtown office where we rented space, because the building was to be razed as a part of the renovation process which is eternal to Chicago. After preliminary investigation we realized that the exorbitantly high Loop rents would prove impossible to meet continually.

The staff at the Tuesday meeting held an extended time for sharing the problem with God. Rarely did we pray regarding finances or physical provisions, having made it a definite policy to trust God, so these moments centered around a personal examination of our relationship before Him to determine whether our attitudes were proper. The Zion experiment was in its final weeks and we were all pretty ragged. At the conclusion, I remember Al saying, "You know, guys, I think we got through." I hoped so, because we were certainly at the end of our rope.

That afternoon I called Mr. Peick at the Union Hall to inquire if there would possibly be office space somewhere in the complex of properties the Teamsters owned on the near west side. Stating that he was busy at the moment, he asked me to come the next morning. When I arrived he took me to a large office in a warehouse building in the same block as the Hall where we hold our Sunday services. The address was 321 South Paulina, and the main part of the first floor was a garage where Union leaders parked their cars. The front portion contained a second floor where there was a large open area including two private offices, two washrooms, and two air conditioners.

"Do you think this would work out?" he asked.

It was perfect. Not only was it more suitable to our needs than the present facilities, it would give us proximity to the neighborhood work.

I told Mr. Peick so. Then he asked, "Do you pay rent where you are?"

We certainly did; in fact it was due at that moment.

Without asking how much we paid, he went on, "Well, then this will help you out, Rev. You can have this space free. How soon can you move?"

At that moment I wasn't sure of anything.

"When you get ready to move," he said, "let me know and I'll send some of my men over to give you a hand."

I felt like running back to the staff yelling, "Hey, you guys! Hey, you guys! You'll never guess what happened!" But God, and Mr. Peick, weren't through.

My years of ministry where leadership is keynoted by gentle prodding, inspiration, prayer, and careful direction-setting had not prepared me for the tools of raw power—the command and the order. The common expression around Teamster City is, "If Louie says . . ." I may be one of the few persons who addresses this labor boss as "Mister," which helps to underscore my naïveté about the world of the truckers. During our entire tour we were constantly interrupted by messengers: "Louie, there's a phone call for ya," or "Louie, the secretary sent me to tell ya . . ."

"What you need," I suggested, "is one of those devices that doctors on duty have in hospitals. They buzz when someone needs you." He thought that was a good idea.

"Go get the carpenter," he commanded. "The Rev can't have offices up here without some privacy."

The carpenter came and instructions were given to enclose the stairwell with paneling and a private entrance.

"Follow me. There are some people I want you to meet."

I went downstairs somewhat like an obedient and well-trained puppy. In the vast parking lot we ran into Joey Glimco, head of the Taxi Drivers' Union.

I don't know much about the system of unions in the city, but I had heard the name before—I wasn't sure when. He was aware of the church since the auditorium was directly above his first floor offices.

"I've seen those people going in there on Sunday mornings with their prayer books. You haven't got any of those hippie types," Mr. Glimco commented.

"Oh, yes he does," countered Mr. Peick. "The Rev's got all kinds! How about giving the church a donation?"

It was not a question as much as an irrevocable instruction. We walked to the headquarters of the Taxi Drivers' Union where a check was written for $100.00. Afterward Mr. Peick explained, "Joey's a good man. I think he'd give you the shirt off his back." This characteristic I discovered that morning was common to many of these men, according to Mr. Peick.

When I left, having made a few more calls with Mr. Peick, I had checks in my pocket totaling $800.00.

Taxicab Drivers' Union	$100.00
Local Wine and Liquor Distributors	100.00
Warehouse Truckers	300.00
Teamsters' Local 705	300.00
Total	$800.00

Plus we had been given office space rent free. All this took place less than a day after Al had exclaimed, "Guys, I think we got through." He had been right!

My heart, of course, was indescribably full, and I proceeded to write a letter of thanks to each organization. To the head of the Local Wine and Liquor Distributors Union I included an additional sentence:

Enclosed you will find a book which I think will be of **special** interest to you. Thank you again."

The book was Keith Miller's, "A Taste of New Wine!"

The office area which was provided on that day has proved a real boon to us. Not only is it operative during the week but it does full duty on Sunday. Classes meet in the open area downstairs (which we have been welcomed to use), brunches are often held after the services in an attempt to further acquaintances, and eventually our burgeoning nursery was moved from the ladies lounge to the upstairs office. Furniture is moved around, playpens and rubber toys dragged out of their storage cupboards, and parents drop off babies and toddlers on their way around the block to the Union Hall.

At this time we had also recently taken on a full-time secretary. Marge was a comparatively new Christian of Polish Catholic background who not only reflected the discouragement which the staff had been facing (imagine the exasperation of working with our staff!) but had expressed some quandary about her personal future —that of an attractive single girl soon to face her thirties. While sharing the miracles which had happened at Teamster City I remember saying to her, "Your turn is next, Marge!"

After moving to the new offices she began seeing regularly Doctor Farouk Girgis who was doing residency work at Cook County Hospital and had been attending Circle Church. When he became ill, the new location of the office made it possible for her conveniently to visit him in the nearby hospital every day. We were not surprised when plans for a wedding were announced. God has a wonderful way of dovetailing His answers to many prayers.

Every so often the phone will ring and Marge will say, "Mr. Peick wants to see you." We used to receive these with some trepidation, never certain as to the exactitude of our position, but the calls have been invariably to our benefit.

"I think you need a sign," and we arrived the next Sunday to see that permanent lettering had been painted on the door of the Union Hall:

> Circle Church
> Worship Services 9:30 to 10:30 A.M.
> Discussion Groups 10:45 to 11:45 A.M.

"Mr. Peick wants to see you in his office right away," and I was ushered into the middle of a Teamster policy meeting which took place during the latest strike. The discussion was intriguing to say the least. The Chicago Locals for the second time in a row had held out for a larger salary and benefit increase than had been settled on the national level. (Eventually the strike was decided to the advantage of the Chicago Locals, resulting in forcing a renegotiation of settlements on a national level.)

"Oh, Pastor," said Mr. Peick, "the reason I asked you to come up here was to tell you that the organ we ordered some months back for the church has arrived and is being installed so that you can use it this Sunday."

This unusual relationship with the Teamsters has remained an enigma to some people. Invariably I am asked, "What do you think the man's angle is?" My response in sincerity is that Mr. Peick has a great interest in the neighborhood and wants to encourage our efforts in that geographic location. His concern with the church is genuine. An article was recently run in "Chicago Today" about this affiliation, based on interviews with both myself and Mr. Peick. To my dismay the headline read, "Teamster Boss Gets Religion." (Fortunately, it was written by the labor editor and not by the religious editor.)

Recently learning that Mrs. Peick was ill, I made a hospital visit. Her husband happened to be present and she mentioned the article.

"That bothered me," said Mrs. Peick, "that headline that said 'Teamster Boss Gets Religion.' That's not so. Louie has always been religious!"

Perhaps that lends insight into his motivations. At any rate, I am grateful to him. Since the church began, we have chosen to accept God's working through whatever means He desires to sustain us, and the glimpses into the labor world have been both fascinating and illuminating. It has been a part of my cultural maturing. The only time I have been asked to return a "favor" was when they requested that I say a prayer for the meal at the dedication ceremony for their new multi-million-dollar office building.

We have no contract that insures our future in the Teamsters' facilities, nor have we asked for a guarantee of that kind. Consequently, we have to consider the possibility that none of these arrangements is permanent. What will we do if we have to move? My answer is, "We will face that when it comes."

I am confident that God will provide for us in the future the way He has both in the past and in the present. At any rate it is a very healthy type of insecurity. Too often the church depends so much on her physical crutches, the roof over her head, the new heating system, the adequate Christian Education facilities, that she completely eliminates the need for God. Trusting in her securities and because of their solidity, she is not forced creatively to overcome struggles and obstacles, inconveniences and dilemmas. We are grateful that these insecurities exist.

The first two thirds of 1969 had held major adjustments for us. Zion had drained our energies and finally been allowed to die. The

personalities of the staff were still in the process of meshing. And
I found myself with increased responsibilities in the role of coordinating pastor. It was also during this time that my wife presented me with a third child, Joel David, who chose to be born at
4:00 on Sunday morning.

The birth of this baby climaxed some personal agonies we had
been experiencing. Years before we had deliberately moved into
Chicago, and the indoctrination of urban life had left us with much
of the scorn for suburban living which most city devotees feel. Our
lives and thinking had experienced fantastic transition.

During the first years on the near north side, Karen underwent
tremendous emptiness in her faith. Somehow her early spiritual
training just did not relate to the overwhelming complexities of
urbanity which surrounded us. It was a form of cultural shock to
which most missionaries give testimony as they move in and out of
contrasting patterns of culture. Karen suddenly realized she had
been accepting the faith of others as her own, and the dilemma
was compounded by the great divergencies which existed between
suburban life and the urban setting in which we now found ourselves.

We had moved from Wheaton, Illinois, which is not only in-
sulated by its suburban character but also by its abnormally high
percentage of Christians, to the Old Town Triangle, a historic
section of Chicago where many of the brownstones and grey-
stones were built after the great fire of 1871. Extending due south
from its boundaries is Wells Street, a commercial and night spot
attraction. Lincoln Park and Lake Michigan are its front yard, making the summer atmosphere something like a resort, with bathing
suits and picnic baskets abounding. The Loop—State Street,
Marshall Field & Co., countless parades, and the Civic Center Plaza
with its Picasso (which we enjoy and Randall our son thinks looks
like an anteater)—is only thirteen minutes away by public trans-
portation. The zoo, botanical gardens, the Chicago Historical Society, and Hugh Hefner's mansion are all within walking distance.

At the time we moved there, Old Town was the hippie center of
the city. Drugs were just on the ascendancy, and we began hearing about teen-age runaways, bad LSD trips, the homosexual community, and experiments in communal living. We became used to
beads and leather, long hair and guitars, beards and bare feet, as

well as driving around and around and around on Friday and
Saturday nights for as long as twenty minutes hoping for a chance
at anything resembling a parking spot.

During the 1968 Democratic National Convention when the
Yippies camped at night in Lincoln Park, we watched the rioting
from our apartment and closed the windows to protect ourselves
from tear gas fumes. It was nothing to see our building on the
television coverage. (In the daytime the staff could observe the
confusion in Grand Park from the block where our original offices
were.) We almost felt the police clubs as they met with heads
directly below us, and once we opened our door to frantic banging
and found eight frightened Chicago teens who had been chased
into the cul-de-sac of our courtyard by the authorities. "Those cops
will kill us!" they whispered, eyes wide with amazement. We
quickly ushered them to the back door and down the steps, and
Karen admonished, "Go home and stay out of trouble!"

Earlier, during the riots which followed Martin Luther King's
assassination, we spent night hours listening to sniper fire from
the Cabrini Projects, those settlements of horror which border close
to the Old Town strip. Our children had been picked up by their
grandfather to ride the train with him on his way home from work,
but we didn't want to leave.

The first night of rioting, before the National Guard had been
mustered, our doorbell rang. It was my brother Doug, a surgeon,
who had driven into the city to attend an orthopedic convention. He
became aware of the danger when he saw store windows being
boarded in preventive measures, businesses closed, and the convention canceled on account of the riots.

"Do you kids know what's happening?" he demanded.

We were well aware of it. That very moment we had been
sitting on the kitchen floor with our backs against the door just
listening to the small sharp explosive sounds which we knew
were deadly. Karen had been "junking" with a friend that afternoon—some blocks away—when a truck veered in front of her
car, forcing her to the curb. "Lady, I wouldn't go down that street.
Those people are mad as Hell. They're breaking windows and
setting everything on fire. Go home." She did.

"Don't you think you'd better come with me?" asked Doug.

Frankly I felt safer in our third floor apartment than having to snake my way to Glen Ellyn on an expressway which was under siege, and I declined. At any rate we didn't feel right in running.

Even in the normal course of city living, violence is a possible companion. A woman in the first-floor apartment beneath us was raped late one evening. There is no such thing as an unlocked door. Bicycles were constantly being stolen from the basement, and careful parents don't allow their children to play unattended.

When Randy was expected home from school, a short three-block walk, one of us would start out to meet him even if he was only a few minutes behind schedule. Overanxious parents? Maybe, but we were aware of times when unruly high school students from one of the nearby sections had roamed our neighborhood beating small children, and we were not going to take any chances.

A woman stopped Karen in the lion house at Lincoln Park Zoo as she wheeled the babies in the stroller. "You Nazi. You get out of here and never come back. We don't need Nazis like you. You should go to church, you dirty Nazi, you!" Karen didn't know to whom to appeal first—the stone-faced people on the benches who heard the incident and pretended not to notice, or the barred animals in their cages.

An unruly drunk sits down by you on the bus. Your taxi driver becomes embroiled in a fight with a pedestrian. The essential dignity and privacy and self-determination of mankind is daily violated.

At night you hear the angry voices from unhappy people below you or across the hall, and although you become somewhat accustomed to the cacophony of sirens and horns and traffic, you are aware that the noise never stops. I've often thought that the night echoes the sounds that the day has had no room to receive.

Why then live in the city?

Because you can never escape or become desensitized to the fact that mankind is hurt, that it is crying, that it is dying. You can't forget it. The city won't allow you to.

We found that the city does many things to you. First, it liberates. Because of the tremendous juxtaposition of individual personalities, there is virtually no pressure for conformity. The story was told in "Reader's Digest" about the man who walked down State Street wearing a huge Beefeater bonnet of the type worn by the guards at Buckingham Palace. No one, not one person turned to give him a second look. You can be the strangest of individuals and have a place in the big city.

The second thing the city does is to teach survival. It is a jungle, and to thrive, you learn the tricks which begin with caution. Karen has a very low instinct for self-protection. (Maybe that is why we got so many phone calls from her knowing mother. "Lock your doors. Don't go out alone. Be careful. Don't take any unnecessary chances.") One evening she was asked to give a devotional in a church within walking distance. I was meeting with a committee in our apartment, and she stayed just long enough to make sure that the refreshments were arranged. Leaving our downstairs hall, she was approached by a young man who had been hiding in the shadows made by the bay windows.

"Can you tell me the way to Michigan Avenue?" he asked.

She knew then that she should never have stopped. It was a suspended moment as Karen helplessly realized the man's intentions, knowing that to scream would not bring help from our voice-filled apartment.

"What's that you're carrying?" he asked, eyeing the book in her hand.

"It's a Bible," she explained and proceeded to lay it on thick. "I'm on my way to lead a Bible study. My husband is a pastor."

The man moved away with the impact of all this holiness, then yelled as he ran down La Salle Street, "Tell your pastor husband that he'd better watch out if he wants to keep you around here very long!"

Karen knew she had been intimately protected but asserted that she felt God was trying to teach her a lesson—caution!

We learned to delight, on the other hand, in the ethnic variations. The German and Polish and Latvian communities, for instance, with their lavishly distinct bakeries and delicatessens, and particularly their excellent family restaurants. We have always claimed that just riding the bus is an emotional experience because of the vast array of life which always crowds its aisles—a kind of daily example of Katherine Anne Porter's "Ship of Fools."

"My name is Sophie," explained one little old woman who sat down next to my wife on the bus, and for the next half hour regaled her with a life story. She was a Russian Jewess whose father had sent her to America before the Revolution. She had spent her life as a cleaning woman, raised three sons, and was contented beyond words with her old age.

"I belong to the Green Center. So many friends who are there. You have a beautiful complexion, my dear. How many children do you have? Two! Children are a blessing. Here's my stop. Thank you for the nice chat." And she was gone—a continuation of the daily lessons we were learning about cultures other than our Anglo-Saxon experience.

While the opportunities for learning in a city are immeasurable, and we tried to take advantage of as many as possible—the museums, the Grant Park concerts, the lectures and exhibits—it is this stretching, this exposure, this awareness the people of the city provide which more than compensates for disadvantages and makes urban experience a continually exciting one.

A waitress pauses during a lull in business, sharing an aggravating slice of her afternoon rush hour—her "dese," "dem," "dose," bearing vaguely familiar resemblances to that world of Damon Runyan.

A black woman grabs your wiggling baby on a crowded bus and plops him on her ample lap.

"What will we talk about tonight?" you wonder, having invited the Teamster janitor and his wife for dinner, only to spend an evening which you term a highlight. "If you held Bingo games, Rev, you could make a lot of money. My church used to have them all the time. Why, the nuns would even watch for the cops."

You become aware of the city's gentleness as well as its fierceness. "Here, Sonny, take these peanuts. You can feed the pigeons with them. I used to have a boy. Looked just like yours, mister!"

Karen has a special place in her heart for truckdrivers who will honk at young mothers with windblown hair and sunburned skin, laden with two toddlers, a baby pushed in a stroller, a beachball, a blanket, and the sticky remains of a popsicle. Their whistle is not freshness—it's bravado!

The lessons learned were so numerous it would require another volume to accumulate them all, but essentially we realized we were city people. Consequently, it was with much consternation, crystallized now by the birth of Joel, that we realized we would have to move out of Chicago.

We knew that eventually the Georgian Courts where we lived

were to be evacuated because of scheduled razing. Constantly rising rental rates would make the three-bedroom apartment we now needed prohibitive. At the same time we were not happy with the public school situation. Many north-siders sent their children to private schools, but even with the rebate provided for ministers' children at that time, this was beyond our means. Still, we felt God could provide the solution to these difficulties if He so chose. In fact, Bill Leslie, one of our pastor friends in a vital ministry on the near north side, had moved into the city partly on our advice and had seen God undertake for their needs in every way. Our major difficulty, however, seemed to center around our first-born.

I have done an unusual amount of counseling with children of people in the ministry—missionaries' and preachers' kids and the teen-agers of Bible school professors. At Circle we have seen time and again the resentments and deep disturbances in these young people which have sprung from pressures applied unwisely in childhood, rendering many hopelessly bitter and some frighteningly beyond redemption. I vowed that if the Lord would ever give me children, raising them would be primary—they would never be sacrificed for the sake of "ministry." Our major effort in life would be to raise them wisely, particularly in the early years. Consequently, when we observed disturbing patterns in Randall, some of which we directly attributed to our home in Chicago, we began to adjust to our preestablished priorities.

Randall is an intense child who needs good doses of privacy. This was not to be found in our small apartment which was constantly filled with people, not even in his bedroom which he shared with a sister and now a baby brother. The play courtyard was large, but he was subject to the conflicting rules of twenty sets of parents, none of whom agreed completely with his own. There was the sign which read, "No Ball Playing of Any Kind," the man who swore obscenities at him every time he passed the door, and the cranky lady who threw forgotten toys down from her third-floor back porch ("It could have hit us and hurt us," Melissa exclaimed— the child wondering at the adult's childishness). Then Randall is much like his mother who, although she loves the city and prefers to live there, is aesthetically and privately inclined, and when enough green or inspiration can't be achieved at the Art Institute flees to the country for a half day or an evening, to return renewed.

His public school teacher consulted with us and expressed despair over Randall's behavior. He was obnoxious and belligerent and very difficult to control. Although she believed he was an extremely smart boy, she hinted that she felt his problems were deepseated. (After all, how many kindergartners get kicked out of "Talking Typewriter" class?)

We were well aware of our child's difficulties—we had lived with this intense, strong-willed little being for six years—and concurred with her that he was manifesting certain problems. He had always been a restless sleeper, but for months now he had been waking two or three times a night screaming, uncontrollably afraid. Karen had consulted a pediatrician about certain physical symptoms he had displayed, and after examination the doctor attributed them to psychological needs.

We were fighting for Randy. The only solution, we felt, was to locate a large enough house with a big yard where our ministry of hospitality could be continued without infringing on his privacy. So it was with hope but also with regret and some embarrassment (especially toward Pastor Bill Leslie) that we moved to the near suburb of South Oak Park, where, with the help of my parents, we were able to purchase a house.

From the day we moved in, Randall's nightmares stopped! His behavior pattern improved. And his second grade teacher reports this year that he is at the head of his class and she looks to him to be her example to others.

"Are we going to move from here soon?" he asked recently.

"No, not for a while. Why?"

"Oh, I just like it here better than our old house. I'm glad we're not going to move."

Despite our apprehension about leaving (deserting?) the city, the decision has worked to our advantage. We are centrally located and accessible to the congregation by the nearby Eisenhower Expressway and by the elevated train with a stop a block and a half from our house. ("Parking was really a problem down in the Old Town area," a friend confided as though we had probably been unaware of it.) We are actually closer now to the office and the Union Hall. We can accommodate larger groups, with room for many to meet at one time. The yard has satisfied Karen's longing for "growing things" and the children's need for play.

We have all stretched a bit and relaxed, realizing how tightly wound we had become from matching our family life to the pace of the city. Yet we are aware of human need around us, and that has become a good reminder of the opportunities for curing and for healing wherever the Christian dwells. We look rather longingly at Chicago and are patiently waiting for the time when we can move back in. We are essentially city people.

With the termination of the contract at Zion, the remaining funds —and there was a considerable amount left despite the worrying —were returned to their treasury and in turn donated by them, with the building, to the District offices of the denomination. During the entire experience, the numerical growth at Circle remained almost completely at a standstill. We were around two hundred at the beginning of the project as well as at its end. It had taken a great deal out of us, but we felt that it had been worthwhile, if for no other reason than emphasizing an awareness of how far we had traveled in a few short years and how different we had become from our backgrounds. Possibly, we concluded, we had tried to reproduce before reaching puberty. From now on we would be more relaxed, even if we became larger than we first thought desirable, and just wait to see what God would do with us.

As a part now of the Circle staff, Al Nestor headed up the work with the many visitors who came, and extended his attention particularly to include encouraging in-depth hospitality among the members. We were thrilled when Ka Tong was made an official chaplain at the University of Illinois Circle Campus. Along with this, he decided to begin a master's program in social work, and the church Board in backing him stated that he should make the required arrangements that would also enable him to remain on the staff. Elected to my second full term as president of the Evangelical Ministers' Association of Greater Chicago, I continued plans with the other officers to draw together ministers on a basis more broad than the denominational level. One need not work in the city very long before he begins to think of himself primarily as a Christian. All other classifications are secondary. Therefore, I felt this extra responsibility worthy of the time involved.

As has already been intimated, we began to see numbers of hippie types attending the services on Sunday morning. Bare feet, jeans, and hair—lots and lots of it—imposed additional contrasts on our already divergent group, and were welcome. One particular incident relating to these kids stands out in my mind. A new District Superintendent had been appointed, and on his first visit to us sat directly in front of Brother John, a part of an Old Town coffee house group, sponsored by Inter-Varsity Christian Fellowship, which brought many of these people.

Brother John was unable to sit through a morning without smoking (which never bothered me especially, although we weren't always sure just what he was smoking, and eventually we established a policy that if you had to smoke you should sit in the balcony). On this Sunday morning, the air in the Union Hall was dead, and with each exhalation the smoke settled on the head of our superintendent like a large globe. It would finally disappear only to have the next puff land dead center again. I guess it was a fitting introduction to the incongruities we have come to expect of our Circle experience. We would rather have such a person attend and hear of Christ than stay away because of our unwillingness to accept him on his own terms.

The progress of Circle continued to be fraught with the mobility of our members, a characteristic I both dislike and am grateful for. And when a staff member mentioned that he would be moving, my feelings were all the more intensified. Toward the end of 1969, Mel Warren received an opportunity to work with the Reformed Church of America in the Robert Taylor housing on the south side of the city. These public projects—the largest in the world and until recently possibly influenced as much by the street gangs as by the housing authorities—are a series of sixteen-story high-rises. When they were built they were considered to be the "model of the future," but instead they have become a model of institutionalized horror. The outreach would include reading centers, recreation programs, and especially encouraging the youth with plans for beyond-high-school education.

Mel, more than any other, had challenged our preconceptions of race, and we had made major adjustments in the battlefield of staff forums. An extremely literary person, he had pushed us into areas of reading and thinking that had illuminated our concepts of black history and culture. Because of working with Mel, I have pinpointed differences between what is important to white and to black thinking, and how these varying thought processes determine our approach to problems. While it is more important for whites to be solution-oriented, blacks place a high priority on feeling; they are sensitized to emotional pulls. Often many of the frustrating impasses we faced could be directly attributed to these divergent emphases.

"You don't have enough soul, Baby!" Mel would accuse. And I would counter, "But you just can't approach life that way; you have to be goal-oriented, plot your program, sit down and figure it out . . ." Many things were never resolved, but we achieved a sense of mutual admiration, and a better understanding of how each other ticked.

Perhaps it might be well to share at this point that after Mel left Circle, he staged a demonstration in front of his alma mater, Moody Bible Institute, protesting racial discrimination and shredding his diploma. It was mentioned in the daily press and also received national coverage in "Newsweek" magazine. The point of mentioning this is not to condone or condemn the action, but to illustrate the type of militancy which characterized Mel and often pushed us to the point of reaction, but from which we learned and grew and allowed ourselves to be helped.

It was with reluctance that I saw Mel go, because I doubted whether we could find anyone with corresponding qualities. We did what we had become accustomed to doing—committed the problem to God.

On the Sunday we commissioned Mel with our blessings (another farewell and another and another), Ka Tong came characteristically running (bouncing, leaping, charging) toward me. "We found him! We found him!" he whispered enthusiastically (in theater tones). "We've found the man to replace Mel!"

That Sunday Clarence Hilliard had attended our services for the first time. He had just begun studying at Trinity Seminary in Deerfield, Illinois, and on his first weekend in the area had been invited to Circle Church. Ka Tong had preached and in his Pastor's Class took particular note of this black man whose comments bore a great deal of the militant flavor to which we had become accustomed. Our inquiries revealed that he was interested in locating a church position of some type, so we made arrangements to meet with him during the early part of the week.

We discovered that Clarence was a father in his early forties from Buffalo, New York, and there were nine children in the family. He had been a high school dropout who had pulled himself up educationally with the loyal support of his wife Annie, until he was now acquiring graduate training on the seminary level. He had extensive pastoral experience, and also had headed the committee that pushed for and eventually achieved open housing in Buffalo. He had debated with Malcolm X. He was militantly black, but had achieved a maturity and awareness of his blackness which enabled him to approach our whiteness without the chip on his shoulder we so often encountered. In short, he was ideal.

Clarence had come to study in the Chicago area, hoping that he would be able to find a part-time job, and had committed the matter to God. Ours was the first church he had attended, and it was on the first Sunday the vacancy was open. Once again, God's timing was perfect!

Through Clarence's efforts a committee of interested neighborhood people, the majority of whom did not attend Circle Church, was established. He was very strongly of the opinion that it was ridiculous to go into a deprived area and tell the people what their needs were. In effect it would be saying, "Here we are. Here's what we're going to do for you. Aren't you happy?" implying that these people weren't even intelligent enough to know where they hurt. The first step, in his mind, was to organize a neighborhood voice to let the people state their needs. The primary concern of the people turned out to be their children's education.

One of the women, a salaried liaison between the schools and the community, provided names of youngsters who needed special help. The result was the volunteer tutoring of many children by our congregation. Because we have no building to which the children may come, the tutors have decided to conduct these sessions in the children's homes. This creates unfamiliar blends of contrasting lives, and as far as I know, it is the only program on a church basis throughout the city where the tutoring is done in such a manner. The advantages of such an approach are phenomenal. The child is observed in the environment by which he is influenced, and consequently a better appreciation of his needs is achieved by the tutor. Often the tutor finds himself reaching out to an entire family group.

I have been in situations where Sunday school teachers were

encouraged **not** to visit the homes of the children because of the dangers involved. Of course there is a very real possibility of danger and harm in visiting in neighborhood homes. But the overall reaction of our people who tutor seems to be, "Since when have Christians been afraid for their heads?"

The tutoring is conducted on a friendship basis rather than strictly emphasizing the academic. We are not all qualified teachers in the strict sense of the word, and this developing friendship is initially necessary because so many of these volunteers have little understanding of the difficult backgrounds they are facing. Barbara Kuehn's report exemplifies the two-way learning so many of our people have experienced.

> I have tutored Delores ("Cookie") . . . age 8, . . . since last October. Initially Cookie was hyper-active and extremely undisciplined to the point that tutoring seemed entirely unfruitful. She seemed quite insecure and combative in group situations. She indicated a strong attachment to male figures, especially when the latter attempted to invoke discipline. She particularly rejected any affection from me or other girls, would shrug off a hand the moment it rested on her shoulder. . . . She has been under the care of numerous relatives and an orphanage, but now lives with her grandmother, a very good woman.
>
> I soon discovered, however, that a one-to-one situation in which she could accomplish something made her very responsive. Therefore, from late fall to March our sessions consisted of various projects in my apartment. One day she cooked hamburgers "all by herself" and then made cookies to take home to her grandmother. Wrapping Christmas presents for her relatives with carefully selected paper and ribbon made her almost ecstatic. She became so jubilant at this accomplishment that she actually ran over and kissed me before she could catch herself. This was a joyful moment for me.
>
> We took occasional outings, one time to a Geoffrey ballet in which a black dancer starred. Cookie (quite a dancer herself) was entranced by the dance and especially the star. A Saturday at the Art Institute gave her a real thrill. Another time we went to the top of the Hancock Building. However, I kept outings at a minimum because she often became terribly agitated in groups and crowds. Observing interesting things seemed much less fulfilling than doing things which enhanced her sense of worthwhileness.

In March and April my travel schedule prevented me from seeing much of Cookie. I was relieved, in a way, because we seemed to hit a stagnant period. She was fractious and rebellious; I got tired and impatient. I wondered if the whole thing was a big waste of time, but doggedly determined to fulfill my commitment to finish a school year of tutoring.

But at the end of April . . . Cookie began to pester me to tutor her. "My father is getting me a math tutor because you won't do it. You lose!" This sort of thing. Astonished, I moved to take advantage of the opportunity, struggling to overcome the first obstacle—my dislike of math!

Since May, Cookie and I have worked consistently on math, spelling, and phonics, and on reading Bible stories given her by the church. Usually she has to be forcibly hauled into her chair and made to work, but once she starts, her competitive nature takes hold and she becomes almost ecstatic over a high math score or praise for good spelling. Her initial resistance is really a cover-up to get attention.

We were unable to buy math flashcards and so proceeded to make our own out of bristol board. This turned out to be a good move because of the pride she took in creating them and writing out the problems in magic marker. I discovered use of flashcards is the best way to get her over counting on her fingers—she has to memorize the tables in order to spit out the answers fast enough. The flashcards have also helped me to discern her level of knowledge. Although she wants to do division, she still has trouble with addition and subtraction.

Two weeks ago, Cookie read to me her story about Elijah and the Baal worshipers. To my surprise, she had taken the book to school and practiced in her free time. Not only did she read well, her comprehension was excellent. Her reward was "Good News for Children," which I had been holding back until she completed the other. This had made her very angry, but had aroused her determination to read Elijah in order to get the new book. The new book is now a prized possession which should make profitable summer reading.

A coincidental development during the last two months has been Cookie's growing responsiveness on a personal level. As she has received help with her studies, she has become much more affectionate and responsive to affection. Now she happily accepts a teasing hug or a mock paddling and, at the right times, even being cuddled. One day she called me "mama" by mistake. I believe a positive female identification has begun to take place.

I have benefited a great deal personally from tutoring Cookie. Patience has never been one of my strong suits, and I had spent little time around children. I have learned much about patience, tolerance, firmness, and pride. I now understand how infuriated a mother can feel when her child purposely defies her in public. How easy—and inexcusable—it would be to behave childishly in return. While Cookie often ran circles about me in initial months, I have learned gradually how to maintain control without being overly strict or indulgent. (I still have a lot to learn on this score.)

I also learned about my own emotional needs. At times I found myself wanting Cookie to meet my needs for appreciation or affection. I realized more clearly that a person must be emotionally mature to be a good parent. Most of all, however, tutoring Cookie has enhanced my own confidence as a woman, and, I hope, future mother, and increased my appreciation for both the joys and demands of this experience.

The school year is over, but my relationship with Cookie seems to be just beginning to blossom. In light of this and Cookie's potential as a person, I plan to continue tutoring her. Cookie is extremely bright, has strong artistic talents and a great desire to succeed when given proper support. She is also quite volatile. I believe an investment in her now could help her make a strong personal contribution as an adult. However, if some of her basic needs are not met, she could become too insecure and emotionally needy to run her life wisely.

We are strictly learners in the neighborhood ministry. So many of our approaches have been of little value, and we are struggling to evaluate the failures and employ our discoveries for positive influence. The city, with its high rate of mobility and oppressive problems fights against us. We are limited by our own lack of understanding and knowledge.

The forces of evil strive mightily against us. Our denomination's camping program graciously made room for children from the neighborhood free of charge. But on the very first day we were horrified when one of our boys drowned there. We had unintentionally added the finality of ultimate grief to the already unbearable brutishness of one family and to the strangely interbound communication of our neighborhood.

Yet, we are learning—learning that one enduring principle seems to be that all overtures must be made with no strings attached. We do what is done in the neighborhood without requiring these people to attend our church. We are learning that the greatest thing we have to offer is our love, which is in essence Christ's. More and more this seems to be what is needed most!

Along with the tutoring program, a children's choir has been attempted, a girls' club, a Boy Scout troop, and cooking and sewing classes. The church helped to supply outfits for each member of the Scouts, and the troop was ably led by an outstanding young man of the congregation, Gaius Berg, who has been loved almost to the point of hero worship by the kids. One Sunday morning they surprised him with a troop leader's outfit they had bought with funds they raised on their own!

We continually receive from these programs as much as we put into them—usually more.

Chapter Eight

I'm not sure I know what a module is.

There were frequent moments in 1970 when, because the problems we were facing seemed to have no answers, we were tempted to exclaim, "That's it! That's the end! Let's quit and say, 'Didn't we have a good time while it lasted?'" We had analyzed the straitened circumstances of "The Church" and worked out conceptual solutions that to us were exciting. We had faced insolvency with faith and had discovered God's abundant wealth and active concern. We had experienced true failure over the Zion project and still learned lessons that were of great value. But the one thing for which all churches wish—growth—was about to kill us!

A considerable amount of attention had been paid to us in both religious periodicals and in local secular publications. The December 1969 issue of "Time" magazine mentioned Circle Church in its Christmas cover story, "Has God Come Back to Life?" This exposure only served to cause greater problems, as it encouraged many visitors who were "just dropping past to see what was going on," as well as those few ardent enthusiasts who had "finally found the place for which they had been looking."

From our inception we had been convinced that a church's effectivenesss is in direct relationship to the amount of spiritual interaction which takes place among its constituents. The result was our determination to make two hundred our numerical ultimate. Our outlook had included plans to break off when this magic number was reached and to continue the same pattern with any further growth. But we had been "burned" with the Zion experiment, and now were reluctant to branch off in any direction. We

174

began to ask, "Well, **would** more people make in-depth relationships impossible?"

The publicity gave us ample opportunity to discover for ourselves, because the church began to spurt in rapid fashion. Within several months we were over three hundred, and in April 1970 we topped four hundred, peaking at four hundred eighty before the school year ended. The growth ran contrary to the entire pattern of inner-city church ministries where not only are congregations dwindling but sanctuary doors are closing permanently. It must be stated that we experienced this growth while continuing our usual pattern of losing members and regulars through job changes, geographic moves, or the termination of schooling. This meant that the increase in size took place in the face of an ever-weakening and decreasing core group who had a firm grasp on our philosophy and original purposes.

If the staff and congregation could have frozen the picture and taken a sabbatical to analyze the changes being encountered, we probably could have discovered satisfactory answers; but that is not the way life works. We had to participate in the midst of series of actions and reactions, making evaluations from the forefront of our confusion. After discussions on a staff and lay-leadership basis, we concluded that the church should not be pushed to branch out again due to its recoil from Zion—we should just let the growth happen, dealing with the problems this presented as they arose. We decided that possibly it was not mandatory that everyone within a congregation know each other by name as much as having many with whom they could associate and interact on deeper levels. We agreed that if interaction ever broke down within the church, we would be diametrically opposed to our philosophy, but consensus determined this had not as yet happened. Committing our future into God's hands, we allowed Him to do with us as He pleased.

Perhaps because of the delay and introspection caused by Zion, the Circle staff was anxious to fly. We were tired of dragging our heels, and when the albatross was cut loose, we wanted to soar again. Yet, the soaring desired was of a spiritual nature. We wanted to **do** things for God, to see victories won, to see problems overcome, to see our faith exercised, to see our city touched. We were personally interested in the people who came to us and determined to minister to their needs. If that brought growth, so be it. Our experience had taught us this would probably be the case, for where individuals are helped the news spreads and people come.

The preaching of this period centered on being willing to let others share our world. In fact, maybe God wanted us to open our windows even wider to let many see what He was doing among us. One of my series dealt with "The Christian, the Church, and Society." Specifically, the purpose sentences were:

> As Christians, we inherit the role of significance in shaping a society.

> The initial sign of renaissance in a society is the commitment of Christ's followers to the life style He taught.

> Our society acutely lacks a Christian vanguard crying out to God for help from a position of need.

> Society can only benefit when a united spirit of advancing God's Kingdom sweeps through the church.

During the last quarter of 1970 the attendance crossed the five hundred mark!

We finally admitted, however, in the midst of real turmoil that size was not as immaterial as we had hoped to make it. A very strong resistance had built up among the membership—they were tired of constantly meeting new people. It was the core group that bore responsibility for what had become the burden of hospitality. When each week you entertained six people in your home in an attempt to develop meaningful friendships, and each Sunday you faced between twenty to forty new first-time visitors—and the pattern was repeated for weeks without let-up—the result could only be pure frustration. The growth was so rapid there wasn't opportunity for the active nucleus to absorb it. Low Sundays were appreciated because at least they afforded a chance to talk to each other, and maybe get in one or two newcomers as well.

As the year wore on, disgruntled feelings began to rise more and more to the surface. Key members, sometimes not even able to articulate why, became dissatisfied. A Board member resigned and left the church, and the staff, whose intentions were honorable as far as we knew, began to endure accusations which stated that we thought only in terms of the grandiose.

I particularly came on the firing line, with a certain number demanding how I could expect them to be involved in playing a role of destiny in terms of the twentieth-century church when they were mired in the minutiae of inscrutable personal problems. A member of several years stated, "I'm tired of students. I just want a church where I can come with my kids and have them taught about Christ." We began to joke and say, "Whereas the charge to view fireworks at staff meetings is $10.00, the fee to attend our tension-laden Board and business meetings should be $50.00!"

Openness was not lacking, indicated by comments such as, "David, I really am beginning to distrust you. I think you want to be another Billy Graham. If you don't stop this trend it will be the death of the church." We were brutally honest, and discovered with amazement that honesty was not the cure-all for every difficulty.

I began to react to criticism which had no positive application, and my irritation did nothing to allay matters. For a goodly number, the growth pattern was not liked. Even less liked was the alternative of splitting off. We couldn't stop the increase because it represented lives with needs. The cries which essentially mounted to "Do something, we don't like the way things are going" only magnified the dilemma.

On top of all of this, here were all those newcomers, thrilled with Circle Church and its philosophy, overwhelmed by the consistency of worshipful services, intrigued by the new experiences of interaction, delighted by the team staff approach, and enthusiastic to say the least. Many of those same people were later to express, "Why, we never dreamed the church was undergoing difficulties. If we had known we would have prayed or tried to help somehow." Yet I am glad they were unaware. Their fresh inspiration deserved its full chance to flower.

A personal attempt was made to stop reacting and refrain from taking defensive postures. I tried to determine if my motives had been of good intent, and finally advanced to the hardest type of self-examination—discovering areas where you have **unintentionally** wronged people for whom you care. It was definitely a year of attrition. I went around humming certain bars from "Camelot," the stage play that was later put on film,

> Don't let it be forgot that **once** there was a spot
> For one brief shining moment that was known as Camelot.

Not intimidated, the staff decided to make a conceptual change and concentrate on the members rather than on the general attenders. It was at this point that we were soon to refind our floundering identity.

In the midst of our difficulties, there was a change in leadership of the officers of the church Board. The position of chairman, decided almost by default as there didn't seem to be anyone else left with the energy to solve our unanswerable conundrums, fell to John Hiltscher. John is a young architect who is making a name for himself in his field, and who along with his wife had been helped by me in personal ministry. Through the year we had become quite close.

After the Board change was made, Laura and John invited Karen and myself to their swinging north side apartment for dessert and discussion regarding the direction of Circle. With John's impressionistic paintings staring down from all walls, with the jungle of plants lurking in the corners, we settled comfortably in the contemporary furniture, and began to poke and probe intellectually.

I must confess my mind was tired. But I was anxious for satisfactory solutions to questions such as these:

How could we insure that each member retain a sense of self-importance in spite of the increase in numbers?

Was there not a better method of absorbing the interested visitors than the at-random assigning of names for hospitality?

Could we solve the problem of the great amount of work being done by a relatively small number of people?

Had we overlooked the value of spreading the ideas we had discovered by means of casual visitors and students?

When could fellowship among the members be extended beyond the 10:45 interaction time?

How could **group** as well as individual use of the gifts of the Holy Spirit be encouraged?

Karen was exhausted with "church talk" and with her role as

devil's advocate. She refused to enter another such conversation (although she did get in her licks when Laura was busy in the kitchen).

The problem centered on finding an adequate way for the people to get a handle on what was happening. Although most of the congregation appeared contented with the Circle program, significant dissatisfaction stemmed from the core group which made up the Board.

"Eliminate the Board!" Karen brightly suggested, pausing in her conversation with Laura which had been centering around current literature.

We discussed the merits of those churches which bend to the dictatorial personality of a strong pastor, and in effect become a rubber stamp to his desires. But this approach was personally repugnant to me. Yet the Board did seem to be the key. As our discussion lingered here, we realized we had an unworkable system—a traditional governing structure in a nontraditional church. Whereas we had changed the entire format of the services to make them meaningful, we had never considered altering the government!

The more we looked at members of the Board, the more we discovered that they had taken on jobs about which they weren't really excited out of feelings of obligation. The financial chairman hated finances! The chairman of the Services Committee certainly wasn't enamored with recruiting ushers, etc. Why weren't they interested?

"Probably the basic reason," John replied, "is that this is not where their abilities are."

"Where are their abilities?"

"Well, in my case," John answered, "I'm interested in the arts."

All of a sudden, lights began flashing in both our minds. Even Karen (who had pretended not to be listening) was immediately drawn into the conversation. We realized we had been guilty of promoting one of the traditional errors we had continually decried —accepting a prescribed structure and then forcing people into that existing mold.

"Why not then have a committee on the arts?" someone demanded, and we were off and running. It was an exciting evening.

What were the spiritual gifts of the people? As we named members, we discovered individuals with proficiencies in dramatics or in writing who had been relegated to teaching a Sunday school class or chairing the membership committee. We looked hard at a whole church of extremely creative people where the development of supernatural gifts of the Holy Spirit was continually preached. But because of adherence to a traditional governing structure, we had not only hindered our philosophy but eliminated the cooperation of gifted people on a group level.

"This person has a gift for counseling. He should be using that within the church. What are your interests, David?"

I answered that I had a consuming desire to see local churches everywhere come alive, and wanted to explore what part mass communications could play in this.

For the first time it seemed that a possible solution for the great dilemmas in which we had become enmeshed was within our grasp. If we could just encourage each individual to analyze the gift he wished to develop, and then put interest areas together, perhaps we could radically alter the source of much dissension.

The concepts which developed from that point onward, which were finalized by the Board and adopted into a new constitution, can be abbreviated into these essential points:

1. Interest groups were to be formed within the church consisting of members who felt they had the same spiritual gift and wanted to work together using it in ministry.

2. The interest groups were referred to as modules. Each member would register his supportive interest in one module, although he would be welcome to be active in as many as he desired. This registration allowed him the privilege of voting in that module and also helped to determine the percentage of church membership each module contained.

3. During any quarter when a module achieved 8 percent of the membership it was allowed to elect a representative to the Church Council.

4. The Church Council, the new governing body of Circle Church, was made up of three corporate officers and the elected representatives who were authorized to express the wishes, needs, and attempts at ministry of their module to the Council.

5. If a large module achieved 16 percent of the membership, its

members were then able to elect two representatives. If a small module did not have as much as 8 percent of the membership, they were welcome to have a nonvoting representative on the Council.

6. Although the modules were initially composed of members, nonmembers were encouraged to perform active roles, and it was through the module that applications for church membership were reviewed and recommended to the Council.

7. Those desiring to change their module registration for a new quarter could do so by informing the church secretary in writing.

Several basic advantages of this system were immediately apparent. Whereas before we had elected a Board which represented the general body but was answerable to no one specifically, this new procedure supplied representative government on its most elemental level. Each council member was now directly responsible to a certain group of individuals which had defined its reason for existence around the common purpose of ministry and developing gifts.

In a church which had grown large, the module system provided a base upon which satisfying interpersonal relationships could be formed. It helped to eliminate that feeling of "I don't know what's going on!" because each module meeting was required to begin with a report of the Council which had met previously. Not only did the module provide information to the membership, but it served as a forum in which ideas and doubts could be expressed and then taken back to the Church Council. Likewise, it solved the cry of "I don't know how to go about meeting other people," by establishing a base for interaction on a sustained level. Also, since new members must apply for membership through a module, old-timers in the interest groups were able to assimilate them into the group without facing the frustration of having too many from which to choose.

Rather than providing a program and cramming unlikely people into obligatory services, we required our membership first to identify their gifts (the key question in choosing a module is not, "What are my needs?" but, "Where has God given me abilities to be of help?"), then to group together, and finally to function in an expression of ministry. The basis of organization is essentially spiritual.

The temptation to politic is always present, but we stress the importance of denying this attitude. For example: A module might be one member short of the required number to insure an 8 percent representation. It would be easy for a "smart" husband to say to his wife, "If you would register in our group we would have enough to elect a representative. You don't even have to attend that much, just sign up and then go to the module of your choice." She must then decide if she is going to agree to be a party to manipulation or if she is going to join the module where she believes God has given her gifts. The purpose of the modules in the church is not to develop power blocks but sensitively and faithfully to provide avenues for the expression of our gifts and to form small supportive groups that will assist in developing these potentials.

There were some expressions of consternation and fear: "What if no one shows an interest in Christian Education, or has the gift of teaching? Who is going to take care of the children? Or what if there is no concern for missions; does this mean there won't be that emphasis in our church?" Our attitude is, "If the Lord has seen fit to form our body minus those who have both concern and gifts in these areas, we'll just have to do without." Fortunately, however, the Holy Spirit has proven quite adept at His system of equitable distribution.

After the revised constitution had been approved by the membership, a nominating committee recommended individuals for election as church officers: President, Secretary, and Treasurer. The existing church Board was dismissed, and after a period of education we essentially said to the membership, "Do your own thing." For a time we were moorless, again cut adrift in uncharted seas.

"What are your interest areas?"

"I think I have undeveloped gifts in dramatics."

"The possible formation of an urban problem module will be discussed in the center of the hall."

"I feel a tremendous concern for couples with marital difficulties and would like to apply my resources in that direction."

"Will those members interested in the role of the family please meet in the south corner of the balcony?"

And so it went, until tentatively, reaching out cautiously, we met in cells with people who were like-minded in concern. Some

groups exploded into an immediate rush of creative ideas which
served as outlet for ministry. Others, particularly where four or
five strong-willed individuals had difficulty in submitting to the
domination of the group, floundered for a while seeking common
areas of agreement and establishing ground rules for interaction.
Finally the modules solidified, registration was taken, and representatives elected.

Basically, nine modules formed, most of which were large
enough to elect a Council member. Some are specialized while
others play an umbrella role for various functions. Alphabetically
they are Arts, Family, International Outreach, Literature, Mass Communications, Music, Students, Urban, and Ushering. At the time
of this writing we have been functioning in the system for six
months. What has been accomplished in that period will perhaps
indicate why my inclinations toward the module arrangement are
so favorable.

The Arts Module

The history of the artist within the church has been characterized
by alienation. The psychiatrist Rollo May, in his book "Love and
Will" states that the artist and the neurotic are the prophets in society—being years ahead of it in their interpretation of its direction.
The difference between them is that the artist has an outlet for his
prophetic vision while the neurotic has none. The historic dis-
enchantment on the part of the church toward the artist in its midst,
the tendency to view with disdain what it interprets as "bohemian,"
have rendered the church impotent to be in the forefront of societal
change. Consequently it is continually in a state of reaction to
problems which are twenty years old and stale. May asserts that in
order for the church to perform the desired pacesetter role, it must
become a shelter for the artist and encourage his creative functioning.

It is an intriguing theory, and probably greatly factual. I know of
very few churches that have a committee on the arts. In fact the
general attitude of conservatives toward theater, literature, painting,
cinematography, etc., has been to classify all or parts of them as
"evil." Consequently, because we have anesthetized ourselves

against the corruption of these forms, we have also tragically refused to be a part of the prophetic inspiration which they afford.

The evangelical is eons behind in his approach in these areas. Because of lack of exposure, the Christian writer, dramatist, filmmaker, is pathetically, laughably an "also-ran." Our communicative efforts at evangelism through the arts are club-footed, limping, and deformed. We have cloistered, confined, encased, and sealed ourselves from cries of despair. We have created huge vacuums for the impressions which have been filled by secularism, sexism, rationalism, and humanism. The Christian has abdicated his role and driven the artist from the church, with the result that we are pitifully inadequate to present our message of hope and love and faith to a dying world.

At any rate, the Arts Module within Circle Church has soared. Possibly because so many of its members could readily identify their potentials, and because their artistic fervor demands some form of expression, they were instantly ready to function. So often we have said, "Let's do work with dramatics," but were limited by the lack of well-written Christian literature.

A small writer's group formed within the general body of this larger module with plans to criticize one another's work, hold conferences, and provide projects through which talents can be developed. A smaller number is studying dance to determine how this can meaningfully be incorporated into worship. Others with interest in the graphic arts are available to provide material for the overhead and slide projectors, as well as any illustrative visuals needed.

This module recently planned the entire Easter service for the church. They began by encouraging home observances of Passover on Thursday or Good Friday. Research was done into the historical nature and symbolism of this ancient event. Written explanations were given the congregation in the Sunday evening Catch-All. Foods to be served as well as their meanings were suggested, the members were encouraged to open their homes to one another, and they were asked to observe Communion at the end of the evening as Christ had at the Last Supper. The attitude of mind they wanted us to achieve was one of sorrow, as if we were aware of Christ's impending passion, but not of His triumphant resurrection.

The response was overwhelming; well over one hundred participated.

Personally, my heart was moved by the time-honored questions
which our children asked, "Why do we observe Passover? What
is the meaning of bitter herbs mixed with sweet fruit? Why do
we eat flat bread?" The evening ended with Communion. Borrow-
ing an idea from another home group, we lit the individual candles
from a larger one—symbolizing our lives deriving their light from
Christ, the Light of the world. After observing the Lord's Supper,
we extinguished our flames and left without saying a word, our
silent actions depicting Christ's coming death and our deep sorrow.

On Easter Sunday we came to church in a spirit of mourning.
Mimeographed sheets were distributed at the door which discouraged talking during the pre-session and explained to visitors
what had previously occurred. The first part of the service dealt
with heaviness of heart, with our reaction to His death. Members
of the arts group had prepared a ten-minute multi-media presentation utilizing film, slides, the overhead projector, plus sound track,
depicting the realization of Christ's resurrection. Girls from the
church were photographed getting ready in the morning, walking
to a modern-day cemetery, finding the empty grave, and then
running, leaping, exulting with joy at the unbelievable implications of their experience.

As the films ended, footsteps were heard at the back of the
auditorium and the same young women dressed in the clothes we
had seen, came hurrying breathlessly down the aisles. They
huddled in excitement with the staff on the platform before dis-
sembling to spread the word through the audience, "It is true! He
has risen! Pass it on! Jesus Christ is alive!" As we whispered to
each other, we all shared in the excitement which must have
gripped those stunned disciples.

This was followed by a love feast of celebration (after all, there is
such a thing as the culinary arts!). Small groups of ten or twelve
(formed by turning the chairs of every other row around) were
served the contents of large decorated cartons which had been
placed in position earlier that morning. Cheese, grapes and dates,
homemade bread, and juice were shared, as we discussed the
reality of what had been presented that morning and how it related
to our lives.

Following the feast, the sermon stressed the need not to be just momentarily ecstatic but wholeheartedly to do the work of Christ's kingdom. We were reminded that this was what He himself emphasized in His remaining hours on earth after the resurrection.

Another communion service followed, this one celebrated joyfully. A roll was broken and passed, and juice was poured from a common cup into smaller containers. It was a meaningful morning for all of us. And just a sample of what creative people can do if given the opportunity.

After brainstorming services for four years, the staff is more than relieved to have these talented and energetic people sharing that burden. They are scripting readings, writing dramatic presentations, and creating visuals. They are working in conjunction with the Music and Family Modules to provide a summer emphasis for our Christian Education program which will stress music and culminate in a children's recital. They are hoping to publish a manuscript of Circle Church creations which should provide an incentive for our people as well as a symposium for burgeoning abilities. The ideas are limitless, and I am greatly encouraged by their enthusiasm.

The Family Module

The purpose of the Family Module is to provide assistance to the family of Circle Church both on a social and a physical level. Because of the interest of several of its members, it also includes responsibility for our Christian Education program as it pertains specifically to Sunday morning and generally to the home environment which is the most essential framework for a child's spiritual development.

Outstanding financial needs within our congregation have caused this module to establish an emergency fund which does not have to be approved by the monthly Council meeting but is readily available as crises arise. Socials are being planned on a bimonthly basis in order to encourage our geographically widespread families to build closer relationships. A parents' seminar extending over a seven-week period has been planned. The first two weeks will deal with a child's growth development and the following five sessions will specialize in answering the problems of parents in raising children as well as in setting patterns for spiritual training.

The Christian Education program at Circle Church has modified its basic purpose somewhat from the traditional role. Whereas the historic emphasis of Sunday school has been on content, viewing that one hour a week as the primary instrument of biblical training, we feel that **the home setting is more important,** with the church program strictly supplementary.

I am strongly of the opinion that the most satisfactory teaching is done by the parents. If Mom and Dad are excited about what is taking place in their lives spiritually, the multitude of activities which most institutions purvey could practically be eliminated because the contagious spirit of the parent will be picked up by members of the family. The adult who continues to attend a church simply because the youth programs are adequate, even though he himself is bored and dissatisfied, negates the programs' good influence by his inward hostility. Our goal is to help the adult find enjoyment in his faith and then to accent the spiritual home training of his children. Sunday school is supplementary to this basic good.

It would be easy to document the validity of this presupposition not only from recent statements of Christian educators but also from my personal experiences in church youth programs. One example was a basic test on Bible content (referred to earlier in the book) which I administered to high schoolers in a previous place of employment, most of whom had attended Sunday school all their lives. The incentive for achievement was enrollment in an elective class to which capable teachers had been invited to lead discussions on topics of great interest. In order to attend what was called "The Senior Seminar," a score of 50 percent was needed. The questions were third and fourth grade level. Of the eighty or so who took the test, only a few made the required grade. The rest in essence flunked!

Further investigation revealed that the ones who passed were children from homes where consistent biblical training had been maintained through the formative years. Obviously, for the others, all those multiplied hours in Sunday school were not doing what they were supposed to. This experience was the beginning of my change in emphasis.

Viewing Sunday school as supplementary rather than primary necessitated a different approach. We tried first of all to provide parents with information, materials, and training with which to teach spiritual truths. Children's books, handwork projects, even records, were provided each quarter by the church for the parents of every child attending. These were coordinated with the teaching theme that had been chosen for that three-month period. The Family Module's Parents' Seminar is an in-depth continuation of this approach.

Because we believe in the importance of the parent's role, normal stress placed on the teacher-student relationship has diminished, allowing us to change teachers every quarter with ease. Most of our children have a rather adventurous outlook toward this system —"Is this the day we get a new teacher?" Much of the rotation involves the same people—off a quarter, on a quarter. Some prefer to teach for longer periods, but I don't believe we have ever had anyone remain for the traditional year's commitment.

Since each service is purposeful and important, consistently missing one, such as the Interaction Hour, soon produces an acute awareness of misfunction. We prefer having instructors fresh and ready to teach rather than stale from lack of vital contact with others. (Of course there are situations, with which I am familiar, where a person teaches because the alternate adult service is unbearable. That is not one of our problems!) The Children's Church, which meets during the morning service, for youngsters through grade three, has leaders on a shorter two-months basis, because that job seems to be more demanding.

Children without parents or parent substitutes are not allowed to attend Sunday school. It has often been said, "If you get the child, you'll get the parents." We believe the reverse is true. One of the churches where I worked had for many years bused several hundred neighborhood children to Sunday school. It was easy to discover whether the old adage was valid, because most of these children were Negro. But almost no black adults attended either church or Sunday school. In other words, not only were the parents not reached but the children themselves were consistently dropping out at the junior high level.

"What if you have children without parents who want to attend?" we are asked. Our approach may sound cold-hearted—but not if it is realized that for children who do express interest we assign a parental substitute with all the implications attested by that title. We are interested in doing a lasting work in the lives of these little ones rather than taking a here-today-gone-tomorrow approach. Our goal renders our outlook more understandable. On the pragmatic level, we scarcely have physical facilities to care for our own families let alone importing more (hence the development of the neighborhood work).

Our church is one where the adult is of extreme importance. If adults are growing spiritually, the children will reflect that. Even so, I think youngsters are more integrally a part of our program than in any other place of my experience. During the final quarter of last year, our children utilized the Sunday school time to make props for and plan and rehearse an original Christmas play which was presented in the second service in December.

We love to use children in the first service, not hesitating at their duets or rhythm bands or their passing the offering plates. ("Gee! I got a twenty-dollar bill in mine!") They are the world's most aggressive greeters. One Sunday every person who entered the door already had a bulletin in his hand. Walking outside to check, I saw little boys racing each other madly to individuals who came. Some were three quarters of a block away!

International Outreach

Because of my overwhelming impression that the younger generation is reacting against missions, I have been continually surprised to see how many of our collegians have either gone into missionary work or expressed interest in that field. Gradually I have come to realize that they are not expressing disapproval of the concept of the Christian in a foreign setting, but of the traditional role which missions has assumed. Many of today's youth are aggressively evangelistic.

The International Outreach Module in the church is interested in traditional overseas work as well as in the application of the gospel to our modern world. Many of the members of this group have been actively concerned with Ka Tong Gaw about the foreign students in Chicago, feeling that this is an extremely important area of missions. Every other Friday a Bible study for international students is held after dinner in one of their homes.

Module members interrupt conversations after the Sunday services, cassette recorder in hand, looking for friends of Roger and Lan Pfiel who left to teach in Venezuela. "You remember them? Good! Come over here where it's quiet and say a few words of greeting." This tape ministry will also include recorded morning services, if the mass communication module gets its way. A portable bulletin board with recent letters from our members overseas is kept up to date. There is a continued effort to provide a forum during the discussion hours for responsible representatives of missions to present their work and to field questions. These are always well attended.

At Circle we have grappled with the communications gap which seems to hound missions work, especially in light of our increasingly mobile society. Statistics say that the average family moves every three years. This flux seriously impairs true understanding. How can I relate to someone if I don't know him? How can he relate to me if he doesn't know me? That is the crux of the dilemma which faces church mission programs. The missionary may return on furlough and recognize very few in a "turned-over" congregation, and for the new membership to relate to him—well, a smiling face on a prayer card is not sufficient. A "ghost" with a name is not enough. There must be flesh and humanity and struggles and dreams to inspire the praying soul. Our main goal is to maintain an in-depth relationship with the missionaries our people choose to support.

The traditional overseas budget has also tended to encourage depersonalization. Everyone gives to "foreign missions," with so much going to support a family in Peru, a nurse in India, a radio operator on "what field was it?" etc. Prayer letters come to the church office, are posted on the board or included in part in the bulletin—and perhaps the secretary who duplicates them is really informed as to their contents. But it is too easy for the general public to overlook their prayer pleas, and as a whole the relationship between home and field is foggy and indefinite.

We feel more and more that the solution to this situation lies in encouraging individuals to give directly to the missionary rather

than to a church fund. Candidates screened by the module now
present needs to the Circle body, but those who respond financially
make their pledges directly to that individual in care of his mission
organization. (The church office is informed of the pledge for our
own awareness of the response.) If the givers move, they can still
support the missionary, and over the years a steady relationship
grows between the missionary and the individual supporter. The
interest is maintained firsthand through letters.

A further benefit of this system is that members can concentrate
on understanding one or two areas, instead of being overwhelmed
with the incomprehensible needs of the whole world of missions,
to say nothing of varying cultures, governments, climates, histories,
and approaches to ministry. This means we may not have as broad
a base as before—dozens of lights on our missionary map (we don't
even have a missionary map!)—but we feel that we may have a
more valuable and certainly less frustrating relationship with our
missionaries. One person just can't sustain a deep interest in every
mission field; he is forced to be selective in one way or another
by his own limitations. At the same time there is nothing to prevent
a person from carrying partial support for several people or projects, if he's financially able.

We have asked our missionaries to inform us when one of our
members is unable to continue their support and the amount is
carried by a special fund until a new donor can be found to replace the old. In such an arrangement, it is possible that the scope
of the church's overall mission vision will suffer. The module is
attempting to prevent this before it occurs by examining short-
range projects we can support as a congregation—providing money
for a new dormitory or school, for instance, or supporting a tech-
nician from our congregation to fulfill vital functions on a given
field. Despite the difficulties this system of giving may present,
it does eliminate both complicated bookkeeping and also the false
sense of pride that sometimes develops when we measure our
accomplishments by the way they have topped those of the years
before. It also prevents the easy involvement which requires only
vicarious giving.

These ideas may not suit other congregations, but our basically
young, student-oriented, extremely mobile, urban-centered group
has demanded a solution of this kind, and has activated a desire

on the part of the total church to "Help Stamp Out the Communications Gap!"

Literature

Although this module at present only has six members, which is not enough to give it voting representation on the church Council, it has not allowed its aggressiveness to be hindered. The members petitioned the new Council at its first meeting for $200.00 to start a book table. Unsure as to what to do, the Council asked them to come back the next month with a more detailed request of what was needed. The impatient members decided to fund the project out of their own pockets. Immensely successful, the book table is made available to the congregation after the second service and performs vital functions. It greatly facilitates the pastoral suggestions for life response by making recommended literature readily available.

While preaching a series on the millennial reign of Christ, I found George Ladd's book, "The Blessed Hope," a great help. Contacting the Literature Module ahead of time enabled them to have copies available on the morning I mentioned the book from the pulpit—all of which were sold. The book table exposes our congregation to trends in Christian literature. It also makes books accessible to attenders who rarely enter Christian bookstores.

This module has now branched out in its concern to include interest in the interaction groups. Kent Washburn, pastoral intern from Trinity Seminary and a module member, is preparing evaluation questionnaires for the congregation to answer which will help ascertain desired direction as well as provide information for the training of discussion leaders for the months ahead.

Mass Communications

Many of the people whose daily work is involved with the communications media make up the Mass Communications Module. In fact, it contains three couples who each own competitive companies! This group desires to contribute to the great rolling ball of creative ideas which seems to be gathering momentum in the church world, and eventually to have ideas that will come back to Circle as well as go out from her.

They are presently working on taping morning services and making them available in a multitude of ways. We constantly receive requests from members in absentia or who have moved to other places: "Can't you please just send me a cassette? I miss Circle so much—you wouldn't believe it. I would be more than willing to pay for them." The International Outreach Module has requested tapes to be sent to missionaries on the field. Every week brings letters from pastors and laymen asking for help in planning, and the Communications Module can see an area of ministry here. Eventually this group hopes, with the availability of funds, to broadcast edited portions over radio.

Along with requests for tapes, the staff is besieged by individuals who want "just a few hours of your time." It is literally impossible for us to meet with all of them—seminarians, pastors, lay people, college students who want to learn more about our approach—without cheating the congregation whom we serve. Yet the validity of the need is recognized. The Mass Communications Module is in the process of establishing one-day monthly seminars. These will be self-supporting and will provide through tapes, staff, and lay personnel a taste of Circle Church without continually disrupting the everyday work of those involved.

Music Module

Too large to fit comfortably with the other arts, the Music Module has limitless possibilities, particularly since the musical program under Larry Mayfield is such an outstanding part of the church. At the moment the members have taken on the major task of classifying for worship hymns and special numbers which deal with the various attributes of God. As a preaching staff we are continually frustrated either by our lack of knowledge of what is available or what seem to be huge holes in hymnology, with no hymns of praise for many of God's qualities. After the cataloging is complete we are hoping these talented people will take it upon themselves to write words and music to help plug some of the holes.

The module and the choir are planning to present an entire hour of original compositions of praise and gratitude. They are beginning also to do something about the deficient musical program of our Christian Education emphasis. We have no pianos or instruments to provide accompaniment for the children's singing, and many of our teachers lament their inadequacies at carrying a tune! So it is with great relief that we are looking forward to some professional and knowledgeable aid at this point.

We are also hoping to form a sub-group composed of people with an interest in the rock sound. We hope by this to make some original contributions to areas which need to be filled with the message of Christ's love through this idiom.

Urban Module

The urban module wanted to center its interests on more than the specific needs of our immediate neighborhood. Consequently, much of its efforts has been put into examining the problems and pressures of living in an urban society. They have given a great deal of attention to the dilemma of housing and are in the process of brainstorming ways to meet areas of needs.

Perhaps this reflects the general attitude of the church. We view ourselves as an "urban" church rather than an "inner-city" church. The latter term is laden with so many connotations—poverty, ghetto life, crime—that it is easy to use the phrase with the hidden motives of getting a sympathetic and condolatory response. In fact, it is easy to feel sorry for yourself if you establish a psychological frame of mind which moans, "We're an inner-city church; it's really hard!" Circle Church is much more than that. We feel that we reflect the entire gamut of city existence from the very poor to the swinging sophisticate. We are heavily weighted on the young side, but that is not so much of our choosing as of occurrence. Consequently we prefer to label ourselves an urban church.

We are hoping that eventually this module will also provide our neighborhood work and Clarence Hilliard with the type of grassroots support and ingenuity that have come from the other modules for corresponding members of the staff.

We feel that this system of church government is providing a

satisfactory answer to the dilemmas which stemmed from our
unusual growth pattern, as well as finally being in line with our
church philosophy. Some people have questioned whether all this
involvement fights with our attempts to eliminate meetings in the
church. It would, if we had to add it to our regular programs. But
fortunately, the flexibility which has been established allows us to
assimilate more activity without using week nights. We use Sunday evenings, that great catch-all, to facilitate our needs, although
some modules by choice get together during the week to allow
their members to attend other interest groups.

Eventually the modules will undoubtedly divide into smaller
more specialized units, as too large a group becomes unworkable.
Some totally new modules will probably emerge as additional
needs are seen and corresponding gifts are brought into play. The
Council is no longer the place where the large amount of work is
being done. Its coordinating role guards against the groups becoming selfish cliques, and encourages their functioning in the context of the good of the total body.

We think we have come a long way. At least the immediate
pressing problems have been solved. If new ones develop when
we catch our breath, we can always try again!

Chapter Nine

Coming full circle in our experiment

The Problems of the Church

Circle Church began as an experiment. It sprang from the concerned hearts of a few members of the younger generation who were perturbed by a lack of personal fulfillment, despite their involvement in church functions, and who refused to allow whatever roles they might have as an influence for change to be negated. Basically the problems we saw with traditional forms and about which we wanted to do something could be defined as follows:

1. **The major meetings are boring, and more than boring, they are inept.** Sunday morning is like Sunday evening is like Wednesday midweek service is like Sunday school class is like the young people's group. The honest man admits, at least to himself, that it would be more interesting to count the offering than to sit through another such repetitive hour. In fact, in one situation, my wife volunteered for Children's Church (which to me was a rather harrowing alternative) rather than allow negative attitudes to continue developing about the morning worship. Members of the younger generation are more direct—they just quit! Traditional evangelistic meetings follow the pattern of the same familiar songs, the same offering appeals, the same musical selections, the same invitational techniques. Chapel services, required attendance for many college students studying at church-related or religious schools, repeat the hackneyed format. Is it any wonder that so many are crying, "Stop! Enough! Enough"?

196

2. There is no evidence of honest self-evaluation. If there are problems it is the fault of the last days, of the younger generation's carnality, of Sunday sports, of the infiltration of anti-Christian philosophies via the communications media, the increased number of false cults; in short, the fault is anywhere but with the church. With great reluctance the question is asked, "What are we doing wrong?" The evidence of this is the way in which honest dissent is dealt with. No forum is provided for the open statements of opinions that disagree; dissent is forced underground into the cells of dissatisfaction which broil in unhappiness while outwardly everyone proclaims, "Wasn't that a blessing?" Unity and uniformity have been traditionally confused, such as in the business meetings where the final vote may be 64 to 43, but someone will invariably ask for 100% unanimity. We have been afraid of any show of differences.

The Christian body is not to be uniform. It is to be united in its desire to accomplish a common task and in its bond of love. We are not to conform to each other's image but to the image of Christ, and in so doing we may discover how very different this process makes us from one another. Christ's mind in the believer renders that man truly the individual he was created to be, with thoughts, initiatives, and drives originating from the inspiration of the Holy Spirit—not from the conformity of the group.

The staff and I can give constant testimony to the fact that when we leave the openness of Circle meetings, where tremendous freedom of expression is not only allowed but welcomed, to go into a traditional ecclesiastical setting, we have to make cautious adjustments. Otherwise we are continually in hot water, creating all sorts of disturbing misunderstandings. The church has been tactful for so long, she has forgotten how to be truthful!

I often hear, "Now if you see anything in this program you don't like, we would welcome your evaluations." Hah! I find if I honestly say what I think and feel, most people are upset, become defensive, and react to me personally.

"Well, you have to be careful how you say things." Yet, when I'm careful, no one understands what I am saying. It has been buried in niceness!

3. There is a great clergy-laity gap. No greater proof of this exists than in the magnitude of sermonizing which is both impractical and impersonal. "Be committed!" the man in the pulpit cries.

"Oh, yes, we want to be. To be committed Christians. But how? How? How?"

"Read your Bible and pray!"

"Oh, yes! We must, we must! But our actions don't match our intentions. We need practical help."

"Love your neighbor!"

"Can't you spell out what that means in today's world? Be more specific."

In aloofness, trying to maintain an example of awesome spirituality in the face of his humanness, working to develop a reputation as a biblical expositor, struggling to be an adequate shepherd to the flock, the pastor has unknowingly created unattainable distances.

A strange reversal of roles exists where the laity does the clergy's job in the building—deciding how to run the church, what colors to paint the classrooms, etc—and the clergy does the laity's job outside—calling on the sick, counseling with neighbors, bearing the burden of prayer, etc. Most churches are very strongly centered around a single minister who is "pooped" trying to do all the spiritual ministrations, preach all the messages, win all the victories, fight all the battles.

Poor clergy! Poor laity! We have come a long way from those New Testament types—Stephanas, Priscilla and Aquila, Fortunatus and Zenas, Lydia, Tychichus, Nympha, Luke, Tertius, Onesiphorus, Erastus, Claudia, and all those brethren without whom Paul or Peter could not have performed their apostolic functions.

Of course certain lay people are able to respond in spiritual involvements but not nearly on the level which was intended by the head of the body, Christ. And often the most creative types (those with devastatingly analytical minds or the artist who is quickly frustrated by mundaneness) can find no outlet for their particular expression, and their tremendous merit and value are lost.

4. **The traditional church is overwhelmed by meetings.** I know of one friend who boasted that every night of the church calendar was filled for one month! I guess the idea was to keep the congre-

gation off the streets. As far as I am concerned, it was a pure and
simple case of religious hypertension. Spirituality has too long
been equated with being regular in attendance. A man can be a
vile husband at home, his children reprobate, he may be enmeshed
in business debts; but if he is faithful at all planned meetings, not
missing a night of the missionary conference, he is a spiritual
giant.

Consequently, the church is passing a fatal flaw (like hemophil-
iacs) in her blood stream. The name of the disease is Ingrownness.
She is talking to herself. While the races war and cry for a message
of reconciliation, she is talking to herself. While parents despair of
understanding their rebel offspring, she is talking to herself. While
those offspring grasp for values and meaning and cry, "Revolution!" she is talking to herself. "You must be like I am. You must
do what I do. You dare not do what I don't do. You have to have
the same skin color, wear the same styles, think the same patterns."
Then she looks at the Christian minority she has become in relation
to the population explosion and dares to ask, "Why?"

5. **The church has a strong identification with brick and mortar
and little with people who are hurting within the body.** Unfortunately most parishioners, when they hear the word "church," immediately think of a building. In business meetings people vote
to spend a quarter of a million dollars on a new facility without
blinking an eye, yet they haggle for hours over a several-thousand-
dollar raise for their pastor—when the man far more profoundly
affects a total congregation than the structure. In fact, if a problem
arises (the youth are dropping out), the solution is often building-
centered (raise money for a new Christian Education facility).

Hours can be spent pouring over architect's blueprints or arguing
whether the parking lot should be expanded, when no one has
time to visit the widow (in her affliction) or act as substitute father
to her teen-age boys. The economy may be shaky but thank goodness the mortgage on the new auditorium is almost paid. (A black
church on the south side of town burned down. Too bad, isn't it?)
Moundside Baptist will be holding a special dedicatory service for
their newly installed $4,000 organ. (We gave the old one to a down-
town mission. It wasn't working, but maybe they can find someone
to fix it.)

"It was ludicrous to paint the front of the auditorium a pea green."

"Bill Miller's about ready to quit the church; he can't get the janitor to cooperate in setting up the basement for the boys' club."

"I'm so glad we called that man; they say his church in Pennsylvania was a model of redecoration. I think he'll have a lot of ideas about what to do here."

"The deacons refuse to have small coat hooks screwed into the kindergarten Sunday school walls. They don't want holes to mar the appearance. The children have no place to hang their belongings."

News Report: The members of Orthington Presbyterian Church have requested additional police surveillance, as their building was again vandalized last night. Neighborhood children are suspected.

"You mean they built this place without a recreation hall? How can you have a church without a recreation hall?"

"Let's stand and sing Hymn 45, 'Souls are Dying Every Day.'"

"Our church is the one right in the middle of town, the one with the tall steeple."

The Purpose of the Church

There were other problems but most could be directly attributed to one of these basic headings. Yet, as we complained and shared our grievances, the sudden realization struck us that we were as guilty of omission in our analysis as the traditional church. We were like inept members of the medical profession who pass out medications to treat a fever without identifying the cause of infection—the name of the disease. All the problems we had named were symptoms as opposed to a source. The repetitious and boring services, the lack of honest self-evaluation, the clergy-laity gap, the overwhelming number of meetings, the mixing of priorities where material wants overlord human need—these were clues, nothing more, to an underlying malaise with which no one seemed to be grappling.

That core group, from whom the ideas of Circle Church were to spring, began to realize they would have to probe more deeply. "Does it not seem there is a basic difficulty from which all these other shortcomings stem?" was our question. The answer began to boom loudly and clearly: **The number one problem of the local church is that it has failed to define its reasons for existence, and is consequently malfunctioning.**

"Why do we have a morning service? Why have one in the evening? Why a midweek prayer meeting?" Traditionally the answers are that the morning service is worship, the evening is evangelistic, and we gather at midweek for prayer. Yet, the worship is inundated by nonessentials, little evangelism is being accomplished at night, and the prayer usually ends as bridesmaid to another lecture.

The analysis continues further: "What then is worship? What is evangelism? or prayer? How do these exercises fit into the total of what is felt to be the purpose of a local church? And by the way, what are those purposes? How can they best be accomplished? Are our answers biblical? Does Scripture set a pattern of how a church should operate? What keynoted the vitality of the New Testament community? What is important and what is nonessential? What are our priorities?" In essence, **"What is the local church's reason for existence and how should she function?"**

This is why Christendom is floundering, why the institutionalized church is held in ill-repute, why we are no longer lighting the world, or salting the earth. It all comes back to the local church. She has become directionless, mired in purposelessness, and consequently ineffectual and limited—no longer in the forefront of establishing societal change.

I wish it were possible to enumerate the hours I have spent in seminars, retreats, and conferences with other pastors quietly pursuing this angle of thought. I've made it a point to ask these men casually why they conduct a Sunday evening service. If anyone should know, it would certainly be the clergy. I have never received an immediate answer that was satisfactory, and the majority responded as if to ask the question were "to hit below the belt." Sunday evening services are held because they have always been held, and they follow the same pattern because they have always followed the same pattern.

This lack of definition has resulted in the average church's being trapped in an inflexible methodology. Does every service require music? Is a sermon the best way to fulfill the desired objective of all meetings? How can we encourage more participation on the part of the members? In most cases, even these questions are premature because no one has defined why we have churches to begin with. The resultant methodology of tradition stifles creativity. Boredom enters and flourishes among the congregation. Worst of all, the spontaneous, imaginative, inventive originality which characterizes inspiration of the Holy Spirit is quenched, stifled, garroted by inflexibility.

My background has been in evangelical, fundamental churches, but these later years have included a broad base of experience with clergy from all denominations. I have discovered a commonality of despair in the total church. Catholic priests as well as their communicants vocally denounce major difficulties. Dialogue with men from mainline denominations has convinced me that they are facing the same dilemma. There seems to be an agonizing search for renewal, a cry for primitive Christianity.

After agreeing that the basic problem of the local church was her undefined reasons for existence with a consequent malfunctioning, the original Circle Church group began to search for that purpose. What evolved in our thoughts was a statement which is included in the Circle Church Constitution.

ARTICLE II—PURPOSE AND FUNCTION

The **purpose** of this church is to develop spiritual maturity among its people and to relate the gospel of Christ to its world. The **function** of this church is to conduct corporate services of worship and prayer, to afford opportunity for interaction regarding our Faith, and to help its members make use of the gifts of the Holy Spirit given by God.

This succinct paragraph does not even hint at the months of evaluation which gave it birth. Many similar declarations have been included in other formal constitutions, but the crux of their validity is determined by the extent to which they are executed in function. The philosophy of Circle Church (delineated in Chapter Three) is the outworking of an intense evaluation which evolved both pragmatically and in response to spiritual struggle over the period of two years. During the embryonic phases of our experiment we prearranged that four requirements be present:

1. There must be time within the church for honest interaction

about our faith. If superficial answers to questions are given, they have to be challenged.

2. There must be valid worship. Our individual understanding of God and His majesty must improve through the development of creative forms of corporate praise.

3. There should be a meaningful prayer life on the congregational level. Personal requests must not only be shared but be specific enough for us to know if they have been answered or not.

4. There must be an awareness of the gifts of the Holy Spirit and the role(s) each member is to play in the body. Often it is said, "A very strong emphasis must be maintained in the local church on preaching and teaching the Word." Unfortunately this kind of statement stresses certain gifts and devalues the rest. All gifts are essential. "We feel everyone in the church should be able to tell others about Christ." Here again is an unbalanced emphasis which relegates as unimportant all the other spiritual ministrations. We strongly felt that God must be allowed to speak to and through the body by means of **all** the gifts of the Holy Spirit which includes teaching and preaching and verbally sharing the faith, but renders them no more important than hospitality or artistic expression.

It is reported that D. L. Moody once said, "The world has yet to see what God can do through one man totally given to Him. I determine to be that man!" Those words used to make chills run up and down my spine. But I think now the times call for their alteration, for a change in their emphasis. "The world has yet to see what God can do through a **people** totally given to Him." Yet, on second thought, that isn't really a factual statement; the world did see it once!

The world saw a band of disciples stabilized by three years of dedicated training, fired by the actuality of resurrection, imbued with the breath of the Holy Spirit. It watched them endure fire and sword and cross. It heard them sing in the face of persecution and triumph over death. It stared amazed as they shared bread, gave sustenance, healed physical disabilities, cast out demons. It observed them plod in their humanity, soar in supernatural power. They filled the time with visions and dreams, with hope and inspiration. "You are turning the world upside down!" was the cry.

We wanted to come **full circle** in our experiment, back through

the centuries to the early beginnings, to the newness, to the freshness, to the empowering. Kenneth Strachan, the father of Evange-
lism-in-Depth, the movement which has made great advances in
world outreach, maintained that the strength of any ministry is in
direct proportion to the quality and quantity of involvement on the
part of the members within the organization. The realization that
we are all members endowed with gifts of the Holy Spirit has
given our little group within the megalopolis tremendous incentive.
We are all ministers within the body, hoping to influence our world.

With the determination of purpose, suddenly the other problems
vanished. We have young people running out of our ears. A
moving quotation from Francis Schaeffer's book, "The Church at
the End of the Twentieth Century," aptly describes our situation.

> If the church is what it should be, young people will be
> there. But they will not just "be there"—they will be there
> with the blowing of horns and the clashing of high-sound-
> ing cymbals, and they will come dancing with flowers
> in their hair.*

Boredom has evaporated. Each meeting serves a different function, and we choose to carry out its theme by whatever method
best insures success. Consequently, our service ingredients are
constantly changing. The only inflexible rule we maintain is that
we must allow for resiliency. This openness has laid the groundwork for a tremendous expression of creativity. Searching for new
ways to worship is an exciting venture. Discovering modes of
prayer that are not stereotyped and lack pompousness has directed
us down paths we never realized existed.

Self-analysis

The process of self-evaluation seems to be eternal. We are continually making adjustments, and flexibility is a cornerstone of our
foundation. In fact, there are times when we wish we could turn
the analysis off! It is an exhausting and demanding process, but
one of the essential ingredients to our growth.

---

*Downers Grove, Ill.: Inter-Varsity Press, 1970, p. 107.

The Pastor's Class, the philosophy which stresses the interdependence of every member of Christ's body, the whole general tone of honestly representing ourselves before fellow believers, the emphasis on personal prayer—all of these have helped to reduce the clergy-laity gap. The staff is called by first names— Clarence, Larry, Dave, etc. Counseling, visitation, and other tasks are being performed by lay men and women as well as by the professionals.

Ka Tong had been preaching on spirituality, maintaining that it is determined by the way Christians respond affirmatively to all of the scriptural mandates. A checklist of some thirty items was provided to give examples in which improvement could be made. After the final sermon in the series, he asked three people to tell how they had used the list to help their spiritual growth. One woman said to me later, "You know, when that couple [a husband and wife] shared, I really empathized with them. In fact I remember thinking, 'I'm so glad I came this morning!' We like the staff at Circle, but professionals can't help being professional. I'm thankful for the amount of lay involvement in the services." We seem to have a maximum degree of participation on every level as we all struggle for personal expansion.

Then there is the sharing. . . This intimate and loving fellowship of believers (which we could never have undertaken without first defining our purposes and experimenting with methodology) is by far the most fresh and vital concept to take root in many of our lives. We are finding meaning in the church. We are discovering fulfillment.

Circle Church started in one of the hardest of places—the unyielding granite of an urban center. Yet I am constantly amazed by my brother ministers who tell me, "You had it easy! You began fresh without having to overcome tradition." Maybe it was a wise thing to do, but it was not easy, the evidence of which is the small number of new church works which are being formed within the city proper. I am convinced that **a conventional approach with even the strongest of leaders would not have made it in our setting.** That we have come as far as we have is almost a miracle. God's design as to how the church should function is masterful. We feel the principles we have followed are the key to what has taken place.

Scripture does not concern itself with methods, where most of our reaction centers. Methods will change as needs arise, as society evolves, as history turns. It does concern itself with principle, with purpose. I have a close friend who argues that the church should meet in homes because that was the pattern of the New Testament. I think this is dangerously close to dealing in superficialities. It is not important where the church meets. What is important is that it know why it is meeting and how those answers are rooted in biblical mandates.

If we, as Christ's body, can reestablish our direction, if we can submit to an open study of God's truths and then adapt our approach, **we will grow! There will be renewal!** We will rise from our own ashes, endowed with power like a twentieth-century phoenix.

The Future of Circle Church

What is the future of Circle Church? Only God knows. At present we have a certain amount of security because we can project that we probably won't die tomorrow. But we have also discovered that the principle of insecurity works to the Christian's advantage—he realizes he needs God. We are aware of a total dependence upon the mercies of our Heavenly Father for everything, including the loose change in the petty cash envelope. There is no temptation to rest on the laurels of an efficient superstructure. **We need God!** Whatever we do in the coming days we hope will be steps that push us always beyond our own limitations, for we will be in danger if we ever come to a place of too much security.

Will we ever have a building? Although we have seen the obvious advantages of impermanency, of nonownership, we are not completely closed on this issue. We do realize that the city will never be touched through a continuation of the property-building-mortgage mind set—only by vital Christianity. If we had a structure of our own, it would have to be multi-purpose, with an auditorium that would function more than a few hours a week, certainly without pews. It would have to be community-oriented, perhaps house a performing arts center. Certainly it would not be "a holy place."

Size is a big question mark. We have tapered off from our five hundred and settled into a more comfortable three hundred fifty to four hundred groove. It is interesting to note that some of the post-Zion members are asking, "Have you ever thought of starting a branch work?"

"Once before we talked about it a great deal," I reply.

At the moment the emphasis seems to be on sharing with other churches what has happened in our corporate life, to be honest in our appraisal, to be encouraging in our lessons and successes. This book is a first step, to be followed, we hope, by seminars and a tape ministry. We have seen other works view our example—some in the hesitant copying of ideas (mostly emphasizing methodology), and others starting from scratch with a definition of philosophy.

One example of the latter is the Clearwater Community Church in Florida where people caught the vision from Sherm and Marti Williams, a part of our initial core group who moved out. Beginning at almost the same time as our Zion experiment, it is a successful balancing factor to our problem with Zion. Meeting in a junior college auditorium, using classrooms for discussion groups, pulling a mobile home into a parking lot to function as nursery facilities, they have been a Southern parallel to our Northern experience. We have watched with special interest as their growth has matched ours, because their age group has been ten to twenty years older than our own, with a larger number of "establishment" types— people who are successful in their professions and many who are moneyed. Starting with Circle's pattern, they have now developed their own distinct personality and—a major step in the deep South—they recently made plans to take on a black pastor in an attempt to establish an interracial congregation.

Of course, we have viewed carefully, and with some concern, those who have left the body of our fellowship due to mobility. We have seen seminarians taking their first pastorates imbued with new ideas. (Be receptive to them. Don't squash their enthusiasm for the church.) We have read the returning letters—"You don't know how hard it is to find a place to worship. I'm finally attending a small church where I think I can be somewhat of a positive influence. Please send tapes. The pastor has expressed interest in them." (Don't judge her harshly because of new ideas. She is a wonderful, sincere Christian.) "I think you'll be glad to know, Dave, Glen has decided to go into the ministry. We can't deny what we experienced at Circle and feel there is great validity in the pastorate." (Let them find people who love them. But don't make it too easy.) A couple has started a small church in Manhattan ("Shall we call it Circle Church East?" they joked), and another, one in Michigan (we're glad we encouraged you, but honor your own personality).

Whatever happens at Circle or because of Circle, we hope we will always move out in faith, depending on God for His undergirding hand.

Conversions at Circle Church

All the staff will confess to times of discouragement, and every once in a while, it will center around the lack of conversions. "We aren't seeing people coming to Christ the way we should," someone will complain. This is what we consider to be the ultimate verification of our effectiveness. I can remember leaving a staff meeting in which this topic had been discussed to share what had been happening with another congregation. I took along a slide presentation which had been prepared by one of the photographers in our group.

Click . . . the screen was filled by the face of an international student from the Dominican Republic. He had been invited to Circle Church by the wife of the chaplain at Cook County Hospital. After hearing about an Inter-Varsity Christmas holiday retreat for international students, he expressed a desire to attend. We collected a love offering on the spot that provided for his way. As he walked out the door the following week, he grasped my hand and quietly explained, "I asked Jesus to come into my heart last weekend."

Click . . . a Jewish couple, Ken and Rita, appeared. She had been led to Christ by a woman in the congregation and had begun to explain her conversion to her boyfriend. After an extended period of struggle, he came one morning and stayed for a musical concert in the second hour in which guest artist Dave Boyer sang and gave his testimony.

On Monday evening I received a phone call. "David, I think I have had a peace experience with God." A peace experience? How better to describe the spiritual encounter which occurs when a man yields his life to belief in Christ.

The next week, they came over to our home for a meal and began relating what had happened. "We think we are having vibrations from God." Gulp! One of those kinds! Yet as the conversation continued, I realized they were expressing how God was leading them in His own special way, and confessed that I too had received "vibrations" from God.

Click . . . the face of Mary, a lovely young nurse from Illinois Medical School. After she attended services for several Sundays, I received a call from her. She was under tremendous conviction and had question after question. Would I meet with her that afternoon? I drove over to the Medical Center and spent a couple of hours in discussion in the cafeteria. Mary excused herself to find a box of Kleenexes and used them frequently. Since she didn't feel quite ready to make a commitment, and I prefer to leave the wooing to God, I left her still considering. The next morning I received a call from Kay, another nurse at the Center. Mary had appeared at her door at twelve that night expressing an overwhelming desire to become a Christian. In curlers and pajamas, the girls prayed together.

Click . . . click . . . click . . . the slides continued. Four more girls in nurses' training with three out of the four new Christians.

Click . . . click. One by one the faces of my congregation appeared, exploded in size and amplified before me. "I've seen something different in Chuck since he started coming to Circle, and after coming myself I think a lot of the people there have that same thing. I would like it too."

Click . . . two young girls, one with granny glasses. Close to suicide after experimenting with drugs and in despair, they had phoned Al Nestor. He and Lynn spent the evening with them and helped them discover Christ. "Here," one of them said to a startled friend. "You can have this bag of grass. I don't need it any more. I have God."

Click . . . the face of Pablo, another international student (this time from Peru), a product of Ka Tong's ministry.

Click . . . a young girl of the ghetto, in the tutoring program. She had just recently experienced her new beginning.

We had been seeing conversions on such a continual level that they had almost been overlooked!

The Church Is People

That after all is the story of Circle Church. The church is the people. They are her greatest asset. "You know," confided one visitor, reacting to a particularly introspective morning, "I believe if your people would bother less about trying to find themselves and just get involved in ministry, they would be a lot better off."

"What did you say?" demanded Karen, intensely loyal to the people she loves, when I told her about it later.

"Nothing." (I am learning **my** lessons.)

How, without sounding like I was bragging, could I have told about the Bible studies which have been established in neighborhood groups, about the debates on secular campuses regarding the validity of Christianity in which "our" people have been involved, about the evangelistic thrusts or the "Jesus" booths?

How could I have communicated the number who have gone to the mission field or into faith works?

How could I have told of the calls which say, "Can I help?" or "Have you had an answer yet to the prayer request Rich gave?"

How could I have proven my belief that we have a higher percentage of young men going into the pastorate from our body than the average church?

How could I have shared the loving encounters, the patient mercies, the bearing of burdens?

How could I have told of the children from the ghetto who are being given a chance, of the blind girl who was taken on an apartment hunt that afternoon because she had a need, of the drunk who wandered into the hall on Sunday morning and was lovingly driven to his front doorstep?

How could I make clear the acceptance, the helpful examination, the touch of a hand?

Would the visitor have understood about the explosion of creative gifts, the view of evangelism as a total effort, the participation in new worship forms?

"Nothing," I replied to Karen. "There wasn't time to say it right. So I didn't say anything."

APPENDIX

APPENDIX A

Attributes of God for which we have praised Him in our Service of Worship and Instruction:

He is perfect communication.
He has consistency of personality.
He is creative.
He is eternal.
He is good (with subtopics kind, patient, etc.)
He is holy.
He has a sense of humor.
He is infinite and absolute.
He is immutable.
He is jealous.
He is just.
He is life.

He is light.
He is love.
He is omnipotent.
He is omnipresent.
He is omniscient.
He is personal.
He is sovereign.
He is spirit.
He is trustworthy.
He is truth.
He is unique.
He is unity.
He is wise.

APPENDIX B

Further examples of worship prayers:

"God, today I offer you worship because you are immutable. What you were to my parents, you continue to be to me and will be to my children and eventually to my children's children. How good it is to know you *don't* change in regard to your basic character."

The following prayer offering praise and thanksgiving to God that He is life was given by an expectant mother, Cathy Strokosch.

"Father, You have created a big, wonderful universe; and, at least in our tiny part of it, You have miraculously fused it with something other than mere existence—You have given our world that mysterious element we call LIFE. Though I have difficulty *defining* life, You have provided senses which allow me to *recognize* life. Thank You, Father, for these recognitions, even though they aren't always pleasant.

"Thank You for the vision to see the smile that says, 'I love you,' the long grass which needs to be cut, the tear that says, 'My feelings are hurt.'

"Thank You for being able to hear arguing voices of the children next door; for the postman's, 'Good morning, Mrs.'; for the morning snore that assures me of at least beginning another day with the one I love.

"But, Father, You not only have allowed us to *observe* life, You have graciously shared with us the privilege of actually participating in the *creation* of life. Father, even as You created life because of love, thank you so much for letting me, because of love, be one of these allowed to joyfully say, 'We're expecting. We're expecting life!'"

"Father, all of us are able to recognize life in some way. To many life seems very elusive and not quite within reach. But, Father, because of your great love, some of us are able to enjoy life in abundant proportions. I praise You for sharing life with me, through the love of Your Son and daily through the Holy Spirit. I praise You that Your life has filled me, and that I can be assured that someday our unborn child may also share that life which only you can give."

A final illustration of how God can be worshiped through prayer relates to a morning when we were praising Him that He is communicative—that His life principles are always available to us in Scripture, and we can share our thoughts with Him at anytime without waiting in line. God is never too busy.

The service began with the pianist's playing "The Wonderful World of Dr. Doolittle," as four primary children came to the front with their teacher.

"What was the song you just heard?" she asked.

They knew immediately.

"And what could Dr. Dolittle do that was so special?"

"He could talk to the animals!"

"Could he really?"

"No, it was just a story."

"Can anyone talk to animals?"

"Sure, God can!" (confidently)

"Now, you know we wanted you to say that, but you were asked to think at home this week if there really were times when God talked to animals. Did you come up with anything?"

"He talked to Noah's dove and helped him find the olive branch."

"He talked to the lions when Daniel was in their den."

"What do you think He said to those lions?"

"Shut your mouths!" (laughter from the congregation)

"He told the . . . oops, I forgot . . . uh, He . . ."

"We'll come back to you, Peter. Debbie?"

"God told the ravens to bring food to Eli . . ."

"Oh! I remember! (excitedly) He told the whale to spit Jonah out!" (obviously relieved) "Phew!" (more laughter)

"Okay, Peter; and Debbie says He instructed the ravens to feed Elijah. Let's talk to God and tell Him how pleased we are that He *can* talk to the animals He has made.

"Father, this morning we are telling you how pleased we are that you are perfect in your communication. Not only do you speak to man, but you talk to animals as well. In fact, the Bible teaches us that even the elements of nature, such as the wind, obey your voice. Communication is a very key word in our world today. How grateful . . . Now this morning as I conclude my prayer I am of course pleased that you are able to understand my language, but I also praise you that you are multi-lingual. Hear now, in a fitting climax to this prayer concerning your being communicative, the sounds of many languages from the people of our congregation."

Suddenly the numerous internationals among us began to worship aloud in a good fifteen native tongues, and in the midst of the strangely melodic disharmony came the realization that though we could not understand their praise, God, who is perfect communication, could. As the voices continued for about thirty to forty seconds, suddenly the choir began to sing, "Oh for a thousand tongues to sing My great Redeemer's praise." Every one of us entered into this experience of worship.

APPENDIX C

The theme of the morning service outlined at the beginning of Chapter Four was "Though Christ's promised Second Coming seems long overdue, the wise man prepares for His sure return!" The basic text was taken from the parable dealing with the wise and foolish virgins in Matthew 25. The characteristic of God for which we were praising Him was that He is Light. As a choral "Call to Worship" was sung, two imitation Hebrew clay lamps from the Roman period were lit. (After searching all over the city, I had finally located them at the Oriental Institute on Chicago's south side.) The flames shot up several inches high and were a beautiful visual representation of the words the choir was singing:

> My God, how wonderful thou art,
> Thy majesty how bright,
> How beautiful Thy mercy-seat,
> In depths of burning light!

The two lamps continued to burn during "The Approach to God in Worship" and through a portion of the message.

My intention was for one of the lamps to go out of its own accord during the middle of the sermon, consequently becoming an apt representation of the unpreparedness of the foolish virgins. The lamp did go out as scheduled, which was of course noticed by the congregation. (They were completely unaware of the hours spent that previous Saturday figuring out how the blasted things worked, with puffs of black smoke filling our kitchen.)

When the flame died, I stopped to explain that it had been planned purposely and went on to press the very clear point of Christ's parable— that we as Christians should be prepared. Which did we want to be like— the foolish virgins whose lamps went out because they had not brought enough oil, or the wise virgins who had brought an ample supply of oil to wait for the bridegroom?

Following the sermon, the truth of Christ's return was underscored by a technique which we have come to term as multiple Scripture reading. The New Testament has abundant material which deals with the theme of Christ's return, so abundant that it would have been impossible for one person to have read enough to give the idea of its scope. Yet, we wanted to stress emphatically that very idea of the overwhelming amount of Scripture dealing with the theme of Christ's return. Pragmatically we borrowed a concept of Marshall McCluhan which states the high possibility of a person's being able to understand many voices at one time. Following the sermon one person began to read from the writings of Peter:

> "First of all you must understand this, that scoffers will come in the last days with scoffing, following their own passions and saying, 'Where is the promise of his coming? For ever since the fathers fell asleep, all things have continued as they were from the beginning of creation.' They deliberately ignore this fact. . ."
>
> (2 Peter 3:3-5A)

When the congregation began to get the flavor of this, another person from another part of the auditorium began reading as the first person continued:

> From the writings of Paul.
> "But as to the times and the seasons, brethren, you have no need to have anything written to you. For you yourselves know well that the day of the Lord will come like a thief in the night. When people say, 'There is peace and security.' then sudden destruction will come upon them as travail comes upon a woman with child, and there will be no escape. But you are not in darkness, brethren, for that day to surprise you like a thief."
>
> (1 Thess. 5:1-4)

Another forty-five seconds and a third voice began reading, again while the others continued, from another position:

> From the writings of John.
> "Beloved, we are God's children now; it does not yet appear what we shall be, but we know that when he appears we shall be like him, for we shall see him as he is. And every one who thus hopes in him purifies himself as he is pure."
>
> (1 John 3:2-3)

> " 'Let not your hearts be troubled; believe in God, believe also in me. . . .' "
>
> (John 14:1)

Confusing? Perhaps at first, but then the ear begins to sort out each word, each phrase, and the impression is of Scripture's amplitude in the theme, "Though Christ's Second Coming seems long overdue, the wise man prepares for His sure return." As each New Testament writer was introduced and the medley of voices continued, the choir began to sing, and one by one the voices ceased:

> O Lord Jesus, how long?
> How long ere we shout the glad song?
> Christ returneth! Hallelujah!
> Hallelujah! Amen.
> Hallelujah! Amen.

All this time one light was burning, and the other lamp was without light. I remember well one man, a visitor, was so moved he responded in the only way he knew how, by raising his hand and holding it high for some time.

We moved into "The Response of Obedience" by asking the congregation to meditate silently on the question, "If Christ was soon to return, how would you respond? 'I need time to right matters.' 'I'm so glad.' 'That's something I hadn't counted on.' 'I'm in big trouble.' 'I'm not perfect, but I've been learning to live His way.' If Christ was soon to return, how would you respond?"

After the silent meditation, on behalf of the entire congregation, Mary Lou Lindahl stood and sang:

> My lamps are lit, I'll watch and pray.
> It may be today; it may be today.

Following the suggestions for life response, as one great musical voice, the congregation's words were:

> Lo! He comes with clouds descending,
>   Once for our salvation slain;
> Thousand thousand saints, attending,
>   Swell the triumph of his train:
> Hallelujah! Hallelujah!
>   God appears on earth to reign.

It was a moving morning, the impression of which is very clear to me, even today.

For Further Reading

The Greening of the Church, by Findley B. Edge
A practical how-to book for every local church. New, stimulating techniques for dialogue preaching, book reading, small groups, and Bible study are discussed in detail. The author tells how to recognize your area of personal ministry. (#98083 Quality Paperback)

The Exciting Church: Where They Give Their Money Away, Charlie W. Shedd
Tells the thrilling story of local congregations that are so turned on that they no longer moan about budgets and bills. Here are the biblical principles of stewardship: proven, practical suggestions to increase church giving; unusual plans to use in your church fund-raising campaigns. (#80440 hardback)

The Exciting Church: Where People Really Pray, Charlie W. Shedd
Charlie Shedd's questions about the authentic church, his struggle to learn that prayer was first an opening up to God, rather than

man trying to get through to God. Here, too, is a practical plan through which any church can lead its members into prayer partnership (#80373 hardback)

The Exciting Church: Where They Really Use the Bible, Charlie W. Shedd

A step-by-step plan to let God speak again through his word. Includes a helpful checklist for pastors to keep their preaching biblically relevant . . . patterns for going through the Scriptures . . . practical guidelines for personal-study, for putting the sermon together. (#80384 hardback)

The Gift of Wholeness, Hal L. Edwards

The warmly human story of a modern pilgrim in search of himself . . . and in search of God. **The Gift of Wholeness** will give you a refreshing and very real look at one minister and his ministry— a vulnerable, open kind of life that grows and keeps on growing. (#80377 hardback)

God Loves the Dandelions, Roger A. Fredrikson

Learn how this pastor and his people grew as a body in Christ. A new pastor, Fredrikson discovered leaven in his congregation. Little by little, as people began to give themselves to others, the leaven began to yield and spiritual growth occurred. **God Loves the Dandelions** is an experience alive with potential for you and your church. A great gift for the church library. An affirming account for a small group or class study. (#80399 hardback)

The Invaded Church, Donald G. Bloesch

The historic faith of the church is faced with a growing conflict— a new modernism which tends to accommodate the faith to world values. Here is a thoughtful study of the precise relation of the church to society. A powerful reaffirmation of the supernatural and transcendent dimensions of the Christian faith. (#80376 hardback)

Vision and Betrayal in America, John B. Anderson

Congressman Anderson probes the current crisis in our political process. Anderson does not glibly praise "the American dream," nor does he believe that its death knell should be sounded. He issues a rousing call for individuals to think and act so that this country may once again struggle "to find its very soul." (#80389 hardback)

Yes Is a World, James W. Angell

A rousing welcome into the life of affirmation. This hope-filled book includes chapters such as: Man is Born with Rainbows in His Heart; Not the Postponed Life; Transcendence is a Kiss on the Nose; Dancing on a Battlefield. (#80387 hardback)

Daily Celebration, Volume 1, William Barclay (edited by Denis Duncan)

365 devotional selections for personal or family use. Talks about situations which confront people every day: intolerance, greed, war, loss of faith, marital problems, financial difficulties and many others. (#80258 hardback)

Daily Celebration, Volume 2, William Barclay (edited by Denis Duncan)

365 brief reflections offer inspiration in personal or family reading. Topics include: anger, envy, doubt, pride, marital tension, guilt, forgiveness, and hope. (#80340 hardback)

More Power to You, Lee Hastings Bristol, Jr.

A pointed testament to the fact that the Christian faith makes a difference in the quality of a person's life and the work he accomplishes. Practical suggestions on how to find meaning and strength for daily living. (#80405 hardback)

Tracks of a Fellow Struggler, John R. Claypool

For almost two decades as a pastor, John Claypool participated in the drama of suffering and death—but it was always happening to someone else. But now his own eight-year-old daughter, Laura Lee, was diagnosed as having acute leukemia. John Claypool's personal struggle will help you learn to handle grief in your own life. (#80348 hardback)

Barefoot Days of the Soul, Maxie D. Dunnam

In this "thank you celebration" for what Christ has done and is doing, you will discover how to: gain freedom from the strain of self-effort; break out of the box of beliefs you learned by rote; claim the gift of personal wholeness; become an intimate friend of God; enjoy steady, constant growth in your personal relationships. (#80432 hardback)

New Man . . . New World, Leighton Ford
The purpose of this book is to reaffirm the age-old truth that new men in Christ inevitably create new worlds. This book offers an authentic pattern for life which substitutes faith, hope, excitement —life in Christ—for alienation, confusion, and meaninglessness. (#80132 hardback)

Ephesians: A Positive Affirmation, A. Leonard Griffith
"Ephesians proclaims the message which the church ought to be proclaiming to the world today. I believe that it is God's particular Word for us here and now." Leonard Griffith reveals Ephesians as a positive, affirmative, joyous message to a divided and disordered world. (#80409 hardback)

Drugs At My Door Step, Art Linkletter
Art Linkletter's personal story—timely, poignant, tragic, yet hopeful. Offers piercing observations on the people and forces that make up the drug abuse cycle, and the ways that might be tried to break it. Here is helpful, informed advice for parents, for families, for teachers, ministers, for all concerned adults. (#80335 hardback)

Seven Words of Love, Herbert Lockyer
Focusing on the cross and the words Jesus spoke there as the supreme definition of love, Lockyer offers today's Christian a pattern for a life of devotion and service. The familiar words of Scripture are opened up to illuminate truth in a way that points to a more Christlife and Christ-centered way of life in love. (#80396 hardback)